GOD'S
Unfinished
MASTERPIECE

*If she is ever completed,
the world will end.
It's a dark premonition,
but not one without merit.*

GOD'S Unfinished MASTERPIECE

(Woman)

You can judge the book
by the cover

RICHARD DEXTER RUSSELL

Copyright © 2022 by Richard Dexter Russell.

All rights reserved. No part of this publication may be reproduced, distributed, or transmitted in any form or by any means, including photocopying, recording, or other electronic or mechanical methods, without the prior written permission of the author, except in the case of brief quotations embodied in critical reviews and certain other noncommercial uses permitted by copyright law.

Printed in the United States of America
ISBN 978-1-64133-905-6 (sc)
ISBN 978-1-64133-658-1 (hc)
ISBN 978-1-64133-659-8 (e)

Library of Congress Control Number: 2021920834

01.17.2022

MainSpring Books
5901 W. Century Blvd
Suite 750
Los Angeles, CA, US, 90045

www.mainspringbooks.com

ESV Joshua 1:9
"Have I not commanded you? Be strong and courageous. Do not be frightened, and do not be dismayed, for the Lord your God is with you wherever you go."

ESV Matthew 11:28
"Come to me, all you who are weary and burdened, and I will give you rest."

Isaiah 32 New International Version (NIV)
Punishment for the Women of Jerusalem
The Women of Jerusalem
9 You women who are so complacent,
Rise up and listen to me;
You daughters who feel secure,
Hear what I have to say!

Psalm 13 New International Version (NIV)
Psalm 13[a]
For the director of music. A psalm of David.
1 How long, Lord? Will you forget me forever?
How long will you hide your face from me?
2 How long must I wrestle with my thoughts
and day after day have sorrow in my heart?
How long will my enemy triumph over me?
3 Look on me and answer, Lord my God.
Give light to my eyes, or I will sleep in death,
4 and my enemy will say, "I have overcome him,"
And my foes will rejoice when I fall.
5 But I trust in your unfailing love;
My heart rejoices in your salvation.
6 I will sing the Lord's praise,
For he has been good to me.

How long Lord must I wait oh Lord?
Lord answered,
Haven't you not seen nor heard what I've done
"Let there be light."—GENESIS I, 3.

"There never was a false god, nor was there ever really a false religion, unless you call a child a false man."—MAX MÜLLER.

"Remember who is holding you up"

"Remember who hand you're in."

"She is an avatar that embodies something else within herself."

"With these words, I declare every day is women's day I swear."

"I'm no longer standing in the shadows of man ignorance, because I'm the origin of humanity (Woman). I'm God 's favored".

"Do not live someone else's life and someone else's idea of what womanhood is. Womanhood is you"- Viola Davis.

"The omphalos of the book is about women's."

"Love is always trying."

"Love is always caring and sharing."

"Love is work, and the results is you."

"I am using the gift God given me."

"Are you living or existing."

May all women be a blessing to God?

"Row, Row your boat gently down the stream, merrily, merrily life is better than it seems."

We were not created to just sit, we were created to do something.

"God's words never returned void."

GOD'S UNFINISHED MASTERPIECE. (WOMAN)

THE BOOK IS ABOUT TO BEGIN BRACE YOURSELF!

Table of Contents

Introduction 1

Preface 15

Acknowledgments 21

Dedication 23

Story 1   Based On The Story Of Sarah 27

Story 2   Based On The Story Of Mary 35

Story 3   The Gospel Of Women 43

Story 4   Understand Who She Is 55

Story 5   Co-Creator 69

Story 6   Repentant Sinner 81

Story 7   Woman Courageous And Fearless 93

Story 8   Outstanding Faith 105

Story 9   Strong Portrait Of Biblical Womanhood 115

Story 10   Fearless In Faith And Grace 125

Story 11   Diligent Woman 135

Story 12   The Mother Of All Living 145

INTRODUCTION

THIS BOOK IS A collection of 12 short stories of strong women who embody the characteristics of the most important women in the Holy Bible. Read this book to be reminded of the qualities which made these women worthy of the Kingdom of God. Witness how they have kept their faith despite the struggles they were made to undertake. Their stories are reminders that we may find ourselves in hard situations daily. Faced with challenges we think impossible to surpass, we must always keep our faith and trust in the Lord our God and his promise.

I chose to write the book as a comparison and contrast involving the power and love of women's transitioning from some 3,000 years ago until today. Showing, she's jumping over men of greed and power who have polluted the world for their own profit. The ones who also bought politics, religious leaders, and anyone else who prosper at the expense of the poor.

They wrote their own words in the Holy Books and left her out. But the words in this book are -about her, and for her, but you don't know me, but I know you! Just a week ago something happened in my life which I never expected would happen, that I'll get a chance to write about her once again. What a great blessing for me to enjoy this ride one more time. OMG!

I do believe one of the most dazzling displays that nature offers on any given day is her; she's arcing across the sky of life. Her ephemeral occurrences have captured the human imagination for centuries—leading to a wide array of myths and legends as to what caused her.

There are solid scientific and spiritual principles involved in her creation, many of us would probably struggle to describe exactly what those are. But in my book are guidelines to spiritualism, science-artistry behind her. So you can understand the next time you see her, and maybe understanding she is much more than meets the eye. Here's your chance to learn about her adjournment theories that combined Spirituality and science-artistry that surround the eye's ability to focus on her, as well as how the eyes can transform energy into learning women is Godlikeness.

"We share with God each one."

This Book is the sequel to my first book. Therefore I will continue to sow, and hopefully, you will continue to reap as you read. I know if I write positive things about her, then I will attract and ignite positive things in you and in your thoughts and not negative ones.

I have learned if you sow, you will reap. If you have already read my first book and started practicing its techniques, you are beginning the reaping process and on your way to reaping the benefits. If so, keep reading and recommend these books to everyone for their future adventurous endeavors.

Many of you may think or say this book is the same as "God's Masterpiece Woman." I'll say you are right because the subject matter is no longer a secret after reading the books. Every story is considered Scriptures based as Divine Revelations about women's. To educate and increase your beliefs in God's Masterpiece. So try it, if you dare. :)

In this book, my dear readers, you will learn why a woman is God's designed Masterpiece to be Unfinished. Let me explain my reasoning; in my voice comes words that may seems faint as the light from the distant galaxies, to someone. But to most, I must inform you I've passed my younger years traveling between the stars, learning and unearthing secrets, and now sharing God's wisdom about God's created design (woman).

Women are the most important part of God's greatest design for humanity. She's called mother nature, because she can endure wet and dry seasons, good and bad times. She's compared to the typical four seasons winter, spring, summer, and fall.(Love, spiritual, beautiful and power.)

She's there planting seasons, teaching, neutering and harvesting. Her seed moves throughout each year, and we live through her, as well. In these seasons we learn to depend on and come to expect things out of life. So, yes, you find in my book in our lives we go through seasonal life changes. And we endure because of her grace in God's and her humbleness, willingness to obey.

The narrative of this book is spiritual from my point of view. I am aware that some of her adventures may seem incredible, but they aren't, nevertheless, strictly truthful. I have not exaggerated the truth, but I think society has inflicted on her. But, on the contrary, my descriptions are in line with the truthful facts. I have concealed the names of her, but you know who she is!

I have several-folds motives in writing the book, one it's deemed necessary not only for me but for others too in pursuit of the truth. I wish I was more competent for the tasks I have undertaken. Please excuse my deficiencies in consideration of the circumstance. I'm just a mortal man, trying to decipher her.

I'm sure you are aware there's million of words in the English language: some with simple definitions, some with beautifully precise meanings, and some just simply sound more beautiful when spoken. Words are so much more than a meager compilation of letters; they form sentences, paragraphs, books, and stories. Words are a powerful form of communication for someone who wants to share their message with others. What I have put together is what I have considered the top most beautiful word in any language is (woman).

All things are of God, according to the measurements of spirit in them. And now I see the nearest of all to God is woman. I'm bold in my scripting about her and profoundly happy-go-lucky to write about God's masterpiece because I feel what's being said pleases Jesus Christ when addressing his mother (woman).

I intentionally wrote this book into stories, which will allow readers to take notes after each story. And also for you to get to know her for yourself and live life in the format of love, caring, and learning the meaning to life from God's eyes through her.

In the decades I have lived, I've found the simplest of treasures that everyday traveler-long to discover in life is what God gave us, is her. You may discover her company is worthy of learning because I have felt welcome and loved in ways I never imagined possible.

The insight about her in the book is offered freely, and openly, I asked nothing is returned. But I hope you read each story individually and reflect on it for days at a time. And I'm not trying to convince you one way or another, about GOD'S UNFINISHED MASTERPIECE WOMAN, but think about what has been read before you go to sleep at night. For the next day's search, your soul decided for yourself, does it feel right? Does it make sense to you? If so, read another story; if not, there's no need to concern yourself further.

HEAR YE! HEAR YE! READ ALL ABOUT HER . . .

'Hear ye.' simply means 'hey you, I want you to hear me.' In olden times town criers went around ringing a handbell and shouting out important pieces of information the townsfolk needed to know. During that time, not many people could read and write, but time brings about a change. Therefore I'm the crier of the book about her to gain readers' attention to the GOD'S UNFINISHED MASTERPIECE WOMAN. When it is 'read', I am asking you to read and listen and feel the words.

It's my dire hope you can tell everyone GOD'S UNFINISHED MASTERPIECE WOMAN, is the tongue of everyone is talking about and must be read. I hope I've done enough to ensure I've delivered for the team of two God and woman.

The future is women!

Over half the U.S. population is female, so it's crazy to think that women couldn't vote until 1920 in the USA! The 19th Amendment was the end result of a decades-long suffrage movement, and on November 2 of that same year, more than 8 million women voted in elections for the first time, and she is just beginning. In the year 2020 elected the first woman vice-president and in the year 2024 first woman President of the USA.

Researchers have shown the best way to exercise your mind is by learning something new. Therefore I'm hoping you gather a new understanding while earning points, bragging rights amongst your family and female friends, for a healthy mindset .This book is kind of a guide that motivates you to become the master of your own thinking about her.

God's Unfinished Masterpiece (Woman).

Let's be honest, all the fake news out there is exhausting when it comes to women. It clutters our minds and clouds our focus making it nearly impossible to think positively and get anything done—and now I got you thinking. Isn't there something better I could be doing with my time?

Keep reading!

The books dive into a rich history of traditional historically mindful spiritual women. Throughout the book, many stories discuss different spiritual experiences women encountered, despite the information in the books there is a lot of missing information about the epitome of God's abiding loyalties to women.

So I set out to write two informative educational books helping you to learn something new everyday about women, exciting and worthwhile sharing with family and friends.

I encourage you to embark on this adventure with me packed full of educational values learning something new every day.

The women in the Bible and this book and in early life modeled bravery and resiliency in their life. Therefore women in the book are noteworthy which makes this book trustworthy for all .Women's shares there's personal family story, full of trials, tribulation—love lost and traumatic health issues, and the impact on her family. Read and discover the many ways she weaved hope into family connection, through resilience, love, hope and bravery fostered and grown in her children.

The Bible and my books are educational reading you can dive into. Women serve God's purpose and she revealed interesting religious ideas to us. Women are legitimized in the books and provide a connection to something in the past.

Despite what she had to go through, God still triumphed in her life and used her to eventually bring Jesus into the world.

Once you have finished reading my books, you won't look at a woman and not think about what you have read. That's just the way it is. I'm not bragging just the facts, but I'm bragging somewhat although truth stands alone.

All Scripture is given by inspiration of God, and is profitable for reading, for reproof, for correction, for instruction in righteousness, that the woman of God may be completed, thoroughly equipped for every good deeds, for humanity-sake.

The book is written in women's voices needing to be heard. Therefore women please, don't let your daughters be conditioned from childhood to believe she's not great. And meant to live her lifestyle in a certain way and make her own choices for herself. She doesn't need you to tell her to be great because she'd chosen by God to be great!

Therefore open your ears, mind, heart and enjoy.

My book is a mechanism for you to free yourself from the unbreakable cycle of ignorance about her and for you to find answers to your questions. Some of the most valuable facts you will learn in my book about her might help you get on the right side of life about women. Also if you are interested to learn more facts about her keep reading.

One of the many reasons why I wrote this book is to show women's importance due to their own independence and connection to God. This allowed her to maintain neutrality which, in theory at least, made her and sanctuary accessible to all.

"God knows the number of grains of sand and the extent of the oceans to the seas; rest assured God knows you".

More specifically, in my opinion, women are the oracle between the communication of divine knowledge from God for humanity. But perhaps the most important consultation with God as an intermediary. The stories may vary but the endpoint of each version is perhaps more accurate to describe her as the imparting consultations of divine advisers.

My thought process of selection to write this book was a decision that was devised in my mind and the gift chosen for me. This was really birthed in my mind to write about women from God.

The author tries to connect women by their deeds, not their work. Because work is what you do for yourself and deeds are what you do for others. What makes this book so unique and special is that even with two-years time gap between the first book written and the last book written, there is a consistency of thought and messaging about women's and for women's.

I do feel there is no other book that can match my first and now this book about God's creation woman. But there will always be skepticism but I'm fine with that, what skeptics will learn is that this type of accuracy and consistency could only be accomplished by the hand of God. This book is a close up of all women, and about women.

Quote: "You will learn she's a Masterpiece, because you learned to Master your Peace of mind when it comes to her" By Richard Dexter Russell

It is human nature to be fascinated. For some people, chilling illustrations are a reality check—a reminder that life is not all "man or mens." But, women who have a passionate interest, an exciting obsession, or just something fascinating to behold. No matter your inclination or desire, all great artistry or books about her are worthy, or demand praise. This harrowingly spiritual book is by and juvenile artist will leave you feeling disturbed yet also moved by the subject matter.

The inscription written by the author "I'm no pro." Though I've traveled a significant distance to reach the readers, I hope in my message are letters extended, beyond the intended framework of the reader.

PRESSURING the truth about women—what then? Is there ground for suspecting that all women, in so far a goodness. Men have been incredibly inconsistent, and have failed to understand women. Women's atale, when cut through the rumors and myths, the truth is much more complicated and somehow even more jaw-dropping than her beauty and already-velusious reputation.

Strap in: This book is the story of Women for Women's.

Just hold on because all will make sense at the end of the book.

"GOD MAKES HIS WILL KNOWN, THROUGH ME AS I WRITE THIS IS THE WAY"

African proverb, "History will always glorify the hunter until the lion learns to write." You be the judge, find out for yourself if I'm the hunter or the lion as you read.

Her story has both captivated and significantly challenged me over the years in many ways. Her bravery, faith, and obedience have encouraged me to be a better man . Her name is the woman in the book and in life for her namesake, should be blessed. God shows us a map for our own journey that is uniquely remarkable because of her.

One of the things I adore most about the story is the stories, much like our own. She doesn't have a great position or come from a famous, godly family. She's a widow with no prospects and respect. Yet, God moves so mightily in her storyline and uses her to encourage millions.

If you read the book, and I hope you do, you'll be able to see the fingerprints of God all over her life. You won't see God's voice thunder down like in other stories, or see miraculous happenings that change everything. What you do see is her life being gradually led by a God who she believed in, and at the end, you can look back and see how He orchestrated natural events for His divine glory. There are many things we could learn from the 12, in particular, that are worth mentioning here.

According to studies, expressing oneself through artistry is a difficult task. But I'm hopeful, I was able to capture what's necessarily a portrait in motion as a writer or author, addressing women. I'm hoping my words revealed the most influential pieces of art existing today. As I described her in words as artistry in motion for and about all women. Because she was made by God firstly. But most people don't know they can have her throughout their lives and be blessed, or maybe they do!

The most interesting thing I wanted to share with you is, women more than a transaction. She isn't the means to an end of your book. " Honey, I need something. You are the one who can provide it. So do what I need." In this instance you treat her like a recipe book. You want to cook something. You find the recipe. You follow the recipe to cook the meal. You eat the meal. You put the recipe away and you forget about it until you want to make that meal again. When this happens, she is nothing more than a transaction. This is not what she is all about!

As a writer this is the best reward I could give you as I approached the challenge to gain God and woman approval. From what I gathered she has fallen for heaven's and kept on falling until God caught her. What I've learnt, nothing is more wholesome than to write a story that melts your heart like God's Unfinished Masterpiece Woman.

Well . . . as a writer . . . There's nothing more rewarding than seeing these words written by me in a book about God's Unfinished Masterpiece Woman!

Human history has often not been kind to women. Even when they escaped the strict boundaries society placed on them they were often scorned. Yet there are these 12 women whose achievements are recorded in my book and even brought them praise both then and now.

I wrote the two books as an artist, hopefully, depicted as and Frescoes or Rembrandt painting scenes from the book of Genesis, to Revelation creation. I wanted words to show in detail God's Masterpiece of Creation, and God's Unfinished Masterpiece as figures of her throughout the pages in each of the books.

You will learn the absence of one small preposition can feel like spinning a chair, making scrutiny and disappointment, without her. But with her protective hand on your shoulder and the impression of towering women standing directly behind her beloved child or children, glaring at the bullies.

The books took several years to complete, and the ones you are about to read in context, you might say a job perfectly done. But she will never be completed until God's work is done. A Masterpiece can only be started and finished by the creator, so help me God to ensure I have come close and or at least meet your approval in finishing these books. The most difficult thing was to try and put a face with words when addressing her, but I'm sorry, I could not, I'm only human. But I did have one face in mind as I wrote!

God has instituted the quality of glory in women, parts of God's essence of life and love. The truth is reflected all throughout the book, and all throughout the world in her.

God's Unfinished Masterpiece: Woman

The author Richard Dexter Russell found excitement and delight in the idea, writing about God's Unfinished Masterpiece Woman. The book is written by me, and the wisest man in the world in my personal opinionated-opinion. The book was written to equip the people with wisdom, and there has never been a man more qualified to compose this book other than a God gifted one. Everyone should read this book in order to obtain practical, daily wisdom for how to glorify God in everyday life through God's Unfinished Masterpiece, (Woman).

My dear reader on this date and time, something came through me to you for the purchasing and reading of the 12 stories in the book. I have added blank pages after each story for you to take notes and make your own journal as you read.

"God's given us peace in our struggles in his
UNFINISHED MASTERPIECE WOMAN"

A common prayer request: "O God, let my offspring be a girl: with every beauty in the life of women and girls." It's said: "Happy whose children are girls, and woe unto him whose children aren't girls."

As dust grains found within the space rock—which fell to earth billions of years ago. The oldest of the dust grains were formed in stars that roared to bring life to earth. You don't have to be spiritual to appreciate God's Unfinished Masterpiece, (Woman) you have to know only God put her together and one day will completely finish her.

Most people know some facts about her—but here's more, you should know, she's a gift to humanity by God, her home is in everyone's heart, she was assembled on the timeline of God—but many are unaware she represents Love, goddess and peace and happiness for you. If I could create a statue of her my vision would be In Cuneiform writing carved into stone tablets with a reed stylus. Holding a Bible in her arm, inscribed in it, Christ's birthday in roman numerals and a Cross to show the love of Christ's sacrifice. Inscribed on the pedestal, She's of Godsend, who serves as a symbol of Life Omnipotent Victory Endurance (**L.O.V.E**) (**E.V.O.L**) in her and in the world.

Are you still sleeping outside your dream, then wake up and read and learn. She is rooted in ancient times, according to my studies. She is the recurring theme, which employees of all goodness. That of love (and especially the transformative power of love). Whether it is personal love or love personified in the figure of a hero. She is viewed as a force of nature and demonstrates how humanities evolved.

The title story, GOD'S MASTERPIECE WOMAN, is from when I started my journey as a writer several years back. Some may find this work as juveniles. Well, this is the work and words I was given to share with you. But the more you read and write, the more you learn. I have made many changes because I have evolved in my journey as an author. In this story and all my stories are very close to me, and life is about changing. After all, writing a new story is a new beginning for me, it's like starting a new chapter in my life over and over again, listening to God speak.

My dear reader's this part two to my first book, God's Masterpiece (Woman). Yes, I am still bold in my writing about her, and without her, what else do we have? Yes, I've carried over her supernatural, spiritual abilities, and mystical characteristics of God's personal creation. I feel the wordsmith starting to form so breathe in the thoughts, and ideas come roaring out of me and take hold, so brace yourself, seatbelt faster!

This book is appropriate for young teens and up.

I'm hoping you feel my passion for addressing her in the book, but believe me, you will be inspired. You will be motivated to share our story and be a channel of inspiration to all who read. I do believe I have the power to make someone happy, motivated, and inspired just by reading my book and sharing and passing the book to someone else. In other words, I write with compassion because the world needs more of sharing and caring for others for the kingdom of God.

I spent a lot of time and maybe too much time trying to make it perfect in my head before I put my stories on paper because I'm worried about it being perfect for my readers. So I decided to stop waiting for perfection and do my best with what I have and let God do the rest.

"As I address myself in third person context: And as you struggle forward, remember, it is far better to be exhausted from lots of passionate effort and learning than to be tired of waiting around doing absolutely nothing. You will not discover your greatness in your comfort zone, and I believe that this is something you are aware of.

Lastly, just enjoy the whole experience. Being an author is a privilege that not everyone will have to share. Most authors get lost in the journey to success that they forget the essence of writing, which is to SHARE, INSPIRE, and EDUCATE. Looked back to those days when I was still getting my book together, those sleepless nights, and endless research. You get tired, but you keep on going, and you did that not because you want to get rich out of it, but simply to get people to read it. God's words are like taking medicine. You have to follow the instructions for the healing.

It started out to be guidelines for me to put God's word and my feelings on paper, but soon after, I began to write on my second tablet, yes this is my second tablet because the first one burned out and wouldn't turn on. Therefore my wife bought me a new tablet and here we are.

I began to hope one day to share my triumphant relationship with the unfinished masterpiece with others. My prayer is that God will use my storylines in "GOD'S UNFINISHED MASTERPIECE WOMAN" to educate readers who are in desperate need to know there's hope for the ones who are addicted to stupidity. May the Lord be with you on your journey as you read as Jesus been with me?

"God will never leave or forsake you."

My God bless you and keep you safe on all days and in all your ways.

You are not a body: you are a soul. You are a soul who has a body. It's important to understand that before you define yourself. She's God's Gift for Eternal Life is for Immortality, love, and 'the Fountain of Youth.' Think about it, what is humanity's greatest desire—a greater desire -wealth, fame, true love, or sexual gratifications. All is possible through God and woman! Think about it and be prepared for the food of truth in the words you are about to read. Only if your digestive Tract of reasoning isn't clogged with ignorance, if so you might choke, so stop reading and give the book to someone else.

A CHALLENGE TO THOSE WHO DISAGREE. I am so persuaded in my positional thought, ideas, research, interviews, and God's witnesses blessings in writing about her. And also, confident in the evidence presented, I honestly believe anyone who shares my belief in the authority in the wording will be able to cling to endless torment of ignorance after reading the entire book. "Ascent about her can be a powerful madeleine, bringing up strong memories from years ago."

PREFACE

<u>She is unfinished until God finished her!</u>

GOD NEVER PROMISED YOU anything; any promises you were given were kept by God through many sources, including women.

Through the eyes of my mind come words on paper. Therefore I hope this well-researched book immerses you as you read into the everyday life of women. The author's spiritual imagination, engaging style, and gifted present an intimate and enthralling story of the creation of women.

The book stories portray the creation and evolutionary journeys of the unfinished masterpiece of women, page by page as you read until one word grasps and embraces you. Each paragraph will demonstrate the unity and oneness she possesses with the supreme master vision posted on paper to illustrate who she is.

As you continue to read, more discoveries will be revealed and compiled with unanswered questions you might have and will be answered as you read. I hope you will find an unalienable quench of her importance without bias as you read, as literature should be read.

For the purposes of this book, the word "woman," I'm using in one way. I'm using it to refer to all of which is and where we all become; she is the assertion from the hand of God and the mouth of God.

But with perfect accuracy, I write on my tablet with the light of the floating keyboard, and by the will of God I write, too revealed, women are taking over the world! I reference my insightful encounter with visionary guidance from God, not Twitter, emails, Instagram, snap chat, but by all means, use the sources to get the word out referenced the specific teachings within the book. But keep in mind you have to read it for yourself, and just maybe you will learn something.

To begin, I want to introduce this divine document to you about her. You may have known about her previously as a list of the dos and don'ts. Now it's time for you to examine what unique and diversified documentation of who she really is!

When God finished creating her, she was left on the ground in the wilderness under a large oak tree. When She awakens, she asks, Father, who and what am I? Why am I why I'm here? Why can I only hear you and not see you? Because it's dark, what is dark? It's a day without the light from the sky because it's the night it will be bright in the morning, what is morning? Morning comes after night. What are the things high over my head, that's light? She is the Stars that appear at night unless there are certain clouds and she will continue to shine through.

Then God says in due time, all will become known to you. Like the clouds and the sky, the moon, stars, the Milky Way galaxy, wind, rain, sun, the water ocean, rivers, lakes, animals, birds, insect's, and humans. God, who made all and I created you too. I did so I can return to you and see how you have spread my love throughout the world. There are many reasons why you were left UNFINISHED. This is just one of the most important reasons.

I created her first thing in the morning and awaken -you at night, so when morning comes, you will know light. I created all on-my time, so if anyone tries to figure out how much time it took to create the world and all things exist in the world, they would be guessing. They'll learn nothing is impossible for the great I am, I created all and one for me!

No one in physics can use physics to explain why particles of clouds and stars use in her assembling over-head. But what we can't see is the magical vapor condensing around her, but I'll try to show the mathematical explanation as to why this happens. It is easy to see what happens but explaining why "what" happened is difficult.

So let me explain that she goes beyond the physics of relativity, she was designed to be always desirable and irresistible at the same time, with the intelligence to build institutionalized knowledge and procreate the world. God didn't make her different because we know so little about her; we failed to get God's meaning of her. God, entity's is forever within us, which we all share. Awesome is "what" God awesomeness does!

Throughout my years of living research, meditation, prayers, and interviews in these many years, I will try to explain what I found out. Although God has no limits and time is timeless, and space was set aside to give us her! When words are delivered with conviction, but there is no truth behind any of it in your childlike mind; maybe the words weren't meant for you; that's why you don't understand the why, who, what, where, and how God builds her as unification to God."

Within the guidelines of the builder, I, therefore, try to explain about her, therefore I'll use gravity. I had to define space-time by dissecting formulations in relation to valuing singularity. I not only found, but I also proved space-time by aligning space-time with her. I found the working principles behind her in every discovering there was a newly discovered cosmic occurrence. I found the reason for her and the results of that form, which is womanly.

I found out why God created women to become the building formulating and foundation for the world. I found out why man's ideal of her doesn't apply to the foundation of her. Because no one person can understand her because no person could ever gauge her singularity and see what applies when she goes into a singular model. You will read exactly what happens when the "beauty" is exceeded by knowledge and power to procreate. You will understand why religious, mathematically, and scientifically proven who she truly is.

She is simple but graceful, even if you can't understand her. I make this remark because I am forever told I am a man and too stupid to "understand her," and therefore, I am "unable to understand her." Until I learned there is nothing to understand but God loves us. Because God didn't make her difficult, if God has made her difficult, we could not understand anything about her; trust me when I say thistle. But there is nothing to believe in except the will of God has to assemble here for us to love, respect and Cherish for the rest of our lives.

With one simple question, I will derail your ideas and thoughts about her even if you thought you knew her because I'M the only one who knows her completely. Her proven characteristics are proven time is mass, not weight but mass and time presented by God. I'm going to share a very minor thing you knew but didn't know why and how. She is the force in gravity, igniting all sense the cosmic foundation phenomenally that forms her gravitational field in and around her that draws you into her; that's why she was created first.

God knew when he created her, she would be habitual and therefore making her much-needed for humanity, but most are unable to comprehend. It is pointless to try to explain chemistry to a 5-year-old, but I will try for the sake of humanity. See God created her as his miracle for us, therefore only God can complete her; remember this "GOD DID IT," and it can't be undone!

Some men are still in their childlike mind when it comes to women because the chemical imbalances of ignorance block their own understanding. This is my explanation for their lack of understanding about her. But I hope as they read words will change their thinking. But A child's mind must be developed over time, step by step.

As far as the definition of unfinished is concerned, in my opinion, I am saying the work is finished or not, you be the judge! Thus unfinished work could mean many things."

Understanding the narrative may be incomplete, and the narrative is not properly ordered. Therefore the book is unedited for readers to add plenty more of their personal input. This is our interactive book club! She is the only reason leading us to this unfinished work. I want to create a readership of people with temperamental insight because sometimes they lose interest in the character they are to become. This way, you can gain credibility into yourself and creatively build institutionalized knowledge with an overactive imagination that honors you.

ACKNOWLEDGMENTS

I WANT TO TAKE THIS time to acknowledge God, son, and mother and my wife and mother and all the women in the world. Especially the ones I meet and left on the battle field. Advise each one teach all to keep yourself in God's Love.

Star is born every day in the form of A woman. There's many, as though there are many women. Each star represents her there's many but each shines in different ways. They are different in the ways they shine there shine are blessing every day because one is mine. What they have in common they all shine for God and humanity. if one goes out on earth it returned to the sky and shine and if it goes out in the sky it returned to earth and continued to shine. There light is always bright and shining.

Russell's common prayer request: "O God, let my offspring be a girl: with every beauty in life of a Woman." It said: "Happy whose children are girls, and woe unto whose children aren't girls." "Lord, my prayer remains the same, "Please, show me things for what they really are, that I might not be deceived and dishonor you."

I understand and believe the Divine is neither male nor female. However, to use the pronoun "it" seems inappropriate; therefore, I am opting for the grammatical gender "Woman."

DEDICATION

I dedicate this book to God, and women whom
I wouldn't be entitled to make it without.

I ♥ U 2

THIS BOOK BELONGS TO all women, the original and variously gifted creature the world has ever known and as of God's creation. At any age she scarcely passed their novitiate views, and are still under the direction and discipline of her masters, she won love and power brilliantly alone with his blessings. Just in case you didn't know humanity originated on the African continent at least 300,000 years ago. We know from fossil evidence found and identifies as a woman.

The veil is withdrawn, and I'm taken on the responsibility of presenting her to you in my book. I do this for the sake of any women in bondage and who are maybe suffering from wrongs. The one's ears are too delicate to listen and eyes open and don't see. I do it with the hope of arousing conscientious womenfolks in their sense of duty in the exertions of human influence in society

I dedicate this book to God and women and especially my wife and mother. Without them, you would not be reading this. And to all women I met and left on the battlefield of war and in life and the ones who are about to change everything in the world. She is about to bring politics into a position of her victory, that's only the beginning. Fear not my brother and my sister, marvel at these things you are about to witness, she is destined to reign, it's not rigged! GOD is putting her in position so she can take her place in history where literature left her out!

Let's Began

The crepuscular hour is my favorite time to write, when the sky turns deep red and purple and the noise of the day quiten to a whisper. I picked up my tablet and began to scribe what message has been circulating in my head while sleeping to address God's unfinished masterpiece. I'm only the messenger. More and more, I write. I think I'm getting pretty good at it, and I love starting a new journey in life with the words and work God gives me.

My definition, she is a person with meaningful, motivational thoughts; she is idealistic who has surmounted the institutional intelligence and wisdom of God and the power of His Holyoke. A superior human being with such positive radiance that outshines possibility to change reality, with a smile making everything brighter, better . . . and doing this without a specific interest other than for others. She is a giver of life and a recipient of life by God.

Most people do not really understand women are symbols that merge love and spiritual wisdom, of spiritual connection which is an undeniable hallmark of God for those that came before and after her. She is a Godsend! The more we learn about her, the smaller you feel. Case in point, everyone is descended from her as and common ancestor. That means people scattered all over the world who can trace their lineage back to one woman.

A common belief among individuals is that "There is a special someone made for everyone." There are a lot of women in the world, according to Google search. Around 49.6 percent of the world's population is female, with a total female population of 3,710,295,643. There are 101 men for every 100 women across the globe. At birth, men outnumber women 107 to 100, but the male life span is shorter. She is outnumbered but not outlived!

*"**Something to think about**"!*

Maybe you haven't found the right fit, just keep looking. A woman is a journey you take on your travels to unknown lands, you learn about their differences and encounter a wide range of women at the end of your journey and discover God's seed of beauty. She is not the destination, she's the journey you took to find her.

It2. 7. LAMENTATIONS

12 They say to their mothers, "Where is corn and wine?" when they swooned as the wounded in the streets of the city, when their soul was poured out into their mothers' bosom.

13 What thing shall I take to witness for thee? What thing shall I liken to thee, O daughter of Jerusalem? what shall I equal to thee, that I may comfort thee, O virgin daughter of Zion? for thy breach is great like the sea: who can heal thee?

STORY 1

BASED ON THE STORY OF SARAH

INTRODUCTION

Sarah was beautiful, and both Abraham and Sarah were well aware of it. That is why he asked her to say she is her sister. But God saved them from the king Abimelech. The kings in those days used to take away any woman they liked. The kings treated it as their right.

The biblical name Sarah from my research must have originated in the Middle East, near Palestine, Israel, and the Sea of Galilee. Thus, it's not a western name, although it's very popular among the Christians of u.s., and fairly popular among the jews. I've also learned through research there are Muslim women named Sara (note the spelling). The original name is probably Sara, with both the 'a's pronounced as in the word far. The western version, Sarah, is pronounced with the first 'a' as in the word say, the second 'a' as in the word far, and the 'h,' silent. Sara is a very popular name among the Christians of Kerala in India.

Here are five fast facts about Sarah that will provide an added depth the next time you read Genesis.

1. Sarah's name means "princess."

In Genesis, Sarah's was first named, "Sarai," which in Hebrew means "my lady" or "my princess." Then God named her "Sarah," a similar Hebrew name meaning "lady," "princess," or "noblewoman."

2. She was so beautiful it worried Abraham

When they traveled to Egypt, Abraham said to her, "I know that you are a woman beautiful to behold, and when the Egyptians see you, they will say, 'This is his wife'; then they will kill me, but they will let you live. Say you are my sister, that it may go well with me because of you, and that my life may be spared on your account" (Genesis 12:11-13).

Her beauty was affirmed in Egypt, and she was taken into Pharaoh's harem, where she was protected by God, and the truth about her eventually came out.

3. Sarah and Abraham had a sense of humor (but bad timing)

When God approached Abraham and Sarah about giving birth to a son, both laughed hysterically. Abraham "fell on his face and laughed" while Sarah "laughed to herself" and even tried to deny it. She should know better to try to fool God, who said to her, "No, but you did laugh."

4. She was 90 years old when Isaac was born

Abraham and Sarah were quite old when Sarah was pregnant. There was no natural way possible that they could conceive a child. Abraham exclaims, "Shall a child be born to a man who is a hundred years old? Shall Sarah, who is ninety years old, bear a child?" (Genesis 17:17) She did—and named him Isaac, which means "laughter."

5. Her tomb is still venerated today

Sarah lived to be 127 years old, and her burial is the first one to be mentioned in the Bible. She is buried in the "Cave of the Patriarchs," and traditions say that both Abraham and Sarah (as well as Isaac and Rebekah and Jacob and Leah) are buried there.

God's Unfinished Masterpiece: Woman

http://www.gutenberg.org/files/8710/8710-h/images/012.jpg

THE BURIAL OF SARAH.
Dore Bible Gallery, Vol. 2

STORY #1: Based on the story of Sarah

MEN'S OLIGARCHIC THINKING IS, her body is to be used, not her mind. But what they didn't know is her beauty in itself altogether comparable, with her mind as to shock those who saw her, and converse with her irresistible charm, and her presence, combined with the persuasiveness of her discourse. Her characteristics somehow diffused any negatively about her, because you see something stimulating.

Alexis, one woman who laid the groundwork for women today.

As you read the flushes of morning newspapers of the coming day, read about the social and political advancement in which women had gained traction to bear the mark of the Phoenix of emancipation. The result of the reading may make your home less happy but makes society more holy; when you know the truth. But I challenge the heart and head of any man who knows her and who has learned in time she is the driving force in the education civilization for humanity.

Who could have foreseen the unfolding of history during the last twenty years? But if you stand opposed, the passage of her success of our children will be born in the shadows of institutionalized ignorance. Truth is its own decision-making of the facts.

The character of churches began to change all over the world because of her involvement. Churchgoers are hungry for the Spirit, and with hearts set on the Kingdom, she had left her favorite pew in order to 'be the church' and not 'go to church.' Because of her, more and more, we hear the words, 'good sermon,' and more and more was the love of the mother observed in local assemblies.

Evangelism was occurring across backyard fences instead of from pulpits. Alexis had Grace because she earned it. Grace is a state of being; its love essentially to God and his word. It's also manifesting the divinity within you. It's you effortlessly projecting purity and love into the world, and feeling no fear. The best part is how effortless it rubs off onto others. Grace is you doing God's work on Earth. Grace is sometimes amazing, even to the believers themselves. Her name was given by her mother to significantly please God. My Grace is sufficient: God says it only takes one and one I sent you!

STORY 2

BASED ON THE STORY OF MARY

INTRODUCTION

Scripture References—Matthew 27:56, 61; 28:1; Mark 15:40, 47; 16:1-19; Luke 8:2;24:10; John 19:25; 20:1-18.

The woman is mentioned fourteen times in the gospels, and for references about her, we can clarify what she did and how she did it. A striking feature in eight of the fourteen passages is that Mary is named in connection with other women, but she always heads the list, implying that she occupied the place at the front in service rendered by godly females. In the five times where she has mentioned alone, the connection is with the death and Resurrection of Christ (Mark 16:9; John 20:1, 11, 16, 18). In one instance, her name comes after that of the mother and the aunt of Jesus. She stood close by the cross with these women, but because of their relation to Jesus, it would not have been fitting to put her name before theirs (John 19:25). No woman, however, superseded Mary in her utter devotion to the Master. That's why Mary was and is God's Masterpiece!

MARY MAGDALENE.
http://www.gutenberg.org/files/8710/8710-h/
p1.htm[28/04/11 08:33:14] Dore Bible Gallery, Vol.

1 "And the Lord God said, it is not good that the man should be alone; I will make him a helpmeet for him. And the Lord God caused a deep sleep to fall on Adam, and he slept, and he took one of his ribs, and closed up the flesh instead thereof; And the rib

which the Lord God had taken from man, made he a woman, and brought her unto the man. And Adam said, This is now bone of my bone and flesh of my flesh: she shall be called Woman because she was taken out of man. Therefore shall a man leave his father and mother, and shall cleave unto his wife, and they shall be one flesh." Genesis ii, 18, 21-24. In these few words, the Scriptures narrate the love of God.

STORY #2: Based on the story of Mary

THE FIRST STORY REVOLVES around the life of a woman named Caroline. She and her husband, Rafael, have been married for 20 years, but they never had a child. They prayed and prayed and visited all churches around the world. All their relatives told them to just adopt, but their faith never wavered. On the day of their 21st anniversary, a miracle arrived. Caroline is pregnant. They rejoiced together with their families. Caroline was the most cared for by the woman on earth. Rafael made sure that she has everything she needs. All her food cravings are satisfied.

Finally! Caroline gave birth. That moment when they heard the baby cry was the happiest they have ever been. They named their baby boy Nathan which means God's gift. Nathan grew up to be a healthy baby boy. However, on his 15th birthday, he was diagnosed with Leukemia. Caroline and Rafael were both disheartened. They cannot accept that God gave them a baby only to take him away.

They did all that they could in order to help Nathan heal. They worked overtime to provide for all the pricey medicines. Because of over fatigue and exhaustion, Rafael died. The entire burden was left to Caroline, and she started losing her faith. She blamed God for everything, saying God may be playing some sort of cosmic joke on her family. She avoided the church for a long time. Meanwhile, Nathan's illness became more severe. The doctor said he has six months to live.

Caroline felt hopeless. After going to the doctor, Caroline passed by a church, and something inside her told her it's time to pass her burden to the Lord. As she entered the church, she knelt and prayed. She cried rivers of tears in front of the altar and asked for forgiveness. She asked the Lord to take her son's illness. She promised that she and her son would render their lives for the glory of God. She surrendered everything to the Lord and let the Lord take over her and her son's lives.

The next week after their check-up with the Doctor, a miracle happened. Even the doctors cannot explain it, but the Leukemia is gone. True to her words, they attended church again. Nathan decided to enter the priesthood. Caroline wanted to say no. She will be left all alone. But then she remembered her promise to the Lord. Nathan is a gift from Him, and it is only right for Nathan to dedicate his life to the Lord. She let him enter the priesthood. Many years passed, and Nathan became a priest. On the day of Nathan's first homily, Caroline died in her sleep, at peace, knowing that she's going back to Lord's kingdom.

The story of Caroline is like the story of Mary. They are both examples of unwavering faith. Mary was very young when the angel appeared before her to tell her that she will bear a child. Although Mary knows the consequences of having a child without the sanctity of marriage, she trusted the Lord. Like Mary, Caroline trusted the Lord would hear her prayers. She let the Lord take control of her life and dedicated her life to glorify him.

STORY 3

THE GOSPEL OF WOMEN

INTRODUCTION

Old books, old stories, old judgments, old ideas, old conception lies, and thoughts about women are about to end. However, century's tall tales have been told with senseless lies and exaggerations. But the reading in this story will effectively demolish the preconceived lies told about her. I do feel today we are entering a paradigm shift—the world is changing shape. She has often been muted over the ages, now she becomes the long awaited paradigm shift. As far as life-altering paradoxes go, her effectiveness possesses a strikingly paradoxical enigma that will engulf humanity as a whole.

I have carefully examined the story I have written about women, and I know I'm strictly honest in assembling the words given, and I have found great satisfaction in writing. There is an excellent story written about women, and I have attempted to write another. Whether I have succeeded—fully, partially, or not at all—it's for Woman and God to decide.

Writing this story giving voice to the words is electrified from the first page to last; everything I have written is truthful and factual from my point of view. I can solemnly say the book is free from hypocrisy, falsehood, exaggeration, or compromise; let God be the judge . . .

My hope is the following pages, wherein the creation of a woman is taken as an illustration and will be found useful to the readers and not uninteresting to the reader, but inquisitive ideas and thoughts that God creates an inner purity that cannot be defiled.

And the task I have put before me in this story is to give a fitting understanding in the assembling of women by God. Because I've chosen to have her rise from ashes like a phoenix, and lift her from the pages as you read.

STORY #3: The gospel of women

GOD'S CALLING IS EQUALLY important for women. Women are wonderfully made in God's image and likeness, to be able to bring intimacy and love to the world, in all walks of life. Every single day, she is expected to offer light in the world by loving more people and spreading love. The church is equated to a bride or woman. Its main purpose is to spread love and bind people together as one. This symbolic representation is an indication of God's inner desire for a woman. Jesus Christ is considered as the bridegroom, whose faithfulness is tested by giving up His own life just for the sake of humanity, in repentance of the sins made by His people. In the book of 2 Corinthians 11:2, the author desires to present a virgin wife to only one husband. It simply points to the longing for the uncorrupted nation to one God. Therefore, every woman in this world was created not to be alone. Men, on the other hand, should desire and work hard to capture and win over their wives through self-giving and endless love. Every man has once laid his head in the lap of a woman, even Jesus. Taking care of their wants, needs, desires, and her very wellbeing is also a must. Jesus' love for the church exemplifies the delicate, compassionate, and loving side of a woman. She must be treated right and endowed with compassion to invoke her intimate nature. Every woman has a special intimately, compassionate nature that needs to be cultivated and watered with love, dedication, and respect all the time . . .

In my opinion, no two women are alike; they may share the same similarities, but their personalities are different because they are Unfinished.

The unfinished work of a woman is spreading Love, intimacy, joy sharing, and caring to the world. Over the years, this mission has never ended. It has always been observed and done for the rest of her existence and in every generation. A woman gives forth life with great pain and distress. It is something men could not do and compensate for. The sacrifice is indescribable and inexpressible. The situation at giving birth equates to 20 bones fractured instantly, but with great love, devotion, and attention, women forget the pain and embrace the newborn gift God has blessed them with. From then on, immeasurable love started. The first time in her life, "Out of pain comes love."

A woman is purposely created to endure and overcome tough situations, spread love, and radiate forgiveness. She also becomes a symbol of abiding loyalty and devotion. A perfect example would be Deborah's life, who is employed as a handmaiden in a mansion owned by the Russelle family.

This is her story . . .

Deborah scrubbed every bathroom in the house, cleaned all the rooms and other areas, swept and mopped floors, and assisted every member of the family with everything they needed and wanted.

She worked well, strived hard, and there was never a word she complained about the situation they're in.

"What else could I help you, mother?" Deborah asked.

"Take a break now, Deborah. You have helped me a lot already. You still have to attend to the requests of Mrs. Russelle." The mother replied.

Deborah is an understanding, loving, and caring child of Laura and Nelson. They have been serving the Russell family since she was young. This family is running the biggest telecommunication network in the whole of America. Working for them with commitment and dedication had become their daily routine, for if not because of them, they would have experienced starvation and have not found a second family.

Being the sole child in the family never gave Deborah the reason to be selfish, spoiled, or maladjusted. In fact, she is the total opposite. She was nurtured to be a good and God-fearing daughter, just like what she saw from his parents, loving each other and God altruistically. She was never lonely, for her parents made sure she was filled with attention and affection. She experienced contentment, despite living a very simple life. Other than that, Russelle's family also has an only child. His name is Benedict. He is a charming, courageous, and compassionate boy. He became Dorthy's best friend and best playmate. They both found comfort and trust in each other, even at a young age.

Russell's family is rich, but unlike others, they are so kind and generous. They treated Nelson's family like their own and trusted them more, like no other. Laura worked as a chambermaid, Nelson was their personal driver, and Jade became the handmaiden.

One sunny morning, Mr. Russelle asked Nelson to drive Laura to the market to buy fresh seafood for lunch and sweet treats they wished to eat on that day. The royal family wanted to have an intimate celebration, for they were able to reach the target sales in their telecommunication network business in all of the Americans combined.

Benedict and Deborah were so excited that their parents decided to have a gathering for lunch. That rarely happened to them since the Russell family was used to eating at the most expensive and fanciest restaurants. A few moments later, the ambiance of enthusiasm was changed when they heard a telephone call.

"Hello, this is Mrs. Russelle, how may I help you?"

"Mrs. Russelle, this is Police Officer Miller. Your Bugatti Chiron, with a registration number 124440, was bumped by another car. What is more than worse was, the two people in your car were dead on the spot. We did everything we could, but they did not make it. I am very sorry for the sad news and this tragic event." The police responded.

"W-H-A-A-A-T? This can't be true! You are just making fun of me, right?" Mrs. Smith weepily responded.

The minors were confused about what was happening since tears started to fall down from her eyes.

"What just happened, Mrs. Russelle?" Deborah worriedly asked.

"I am very sorry, Jade. Your parents . . . Laura and Nelson . . . both died in a car accident." Mrs. Smith answered while crying.

"NO ! ! ! My father . . . My mother . . . This is unbelievable and terrifying. Ma . . . Pa . . . Why did you leave me? What am I going to do now that you are both gone?" Jade broke down in tears.

Since Dorthy was still young when her parents died, Mr. and Mrs. Russelle decided to take good care of her, so she stayed in their house. She grew up with Benedict and was able to get a good education from a respectable university. After receiving a degree, she was directly hired by the Russell Company.

Years passed, Mrs. Russelle noticed that something special is going on with Benedict and Jade. She felt that they were just more than friends, much more of a romantic relationship. Worried and fearful she was since they have already chosen Benedict's partner without his consent, she shared her observation with her husband.

"This could not be. We loved Deborah as if she's our own, but she's not destined for our son. She is not for him. What will happen to our legacy? Our business? How will it flourish if Benedict will just choose a degree holder, and without a big name in this industry?" The wife anxiously uttered.

"I know. Even if Deborah has a beautiful heart, she did not meet the qualifications we have for Benedict's soon-to-be wife. Only the daughter of a rival's company is a perfect fit for him. This would expand our business and even bring us to the top." The husband added.

Benedict's parents placed Jade into tough situations like firing her from work without no lawful reason. From then on, the way they treated Deborah became different and cruel. Upon knowing what happened, Benedict bravely confronted his parents and ended up choosing Dorthy over them.

"I thought you loved me. How come our company's sake is still your priority? You were so willing to do everything in exchange for my happiness? Your son's happiness? Deborah has been good to you since she was young. She loved you and cared for you. She treated you like her own parents. How could you do this to her?!" Benedict exclaimed.

"This is for your own good, my son. We were just looking at the better things for you. The daughter of Mr. and Mrs. Lee is a perfect match for you. She is beautiful and classy, well educated, known, and reputable. What else could you ask for?" The parents reacted.

"No! I do not love that woman. I only want Deborah. This decision of yours is not for me. This is for both of you. For your wealth. For your reputation. For your business. You are so unfair."

"How dare you to say that? Are you out of your mind? We are your parents. We know what is best for you. You will regret this, Benedict! You surely will." His parents angrily said.

Benedict abandoned his luxurious life and opted to be with Deborah. They got married and lived a very simple but happy life, far from their parents. They worked hard to provide all their needs. Both of them were employed in small companies and earned just enough to sustain them.

One gloomy afternoon, a concerned friend told them that their parents' company had fallen in debt, most especially because of their illness. The couple was shocked and worried. Since Benedict could not deny that he still loves his parents, he offered himself to taking care of Mr. and Mrs. Russelle. Deborah also wanted to do the same, so she permitted Benedict to visit his parents.

After twenty-five years, Benedict went back to their house. He was happy knowing that he is now in their humble abode. It took years for them to be reunited, hopefully. Benedict was anxious, at the same time, because he did not know if his parents would still accept him or not, after choosing Jade over them. On an antique gold sofa, he saw his Mom and Dad sitting and looking terribly sick. He was so unsure of what to say first, but he bravely approached them.

"Mom . . . Dad . . . How are you? I felt sorry for what happened to you. Allow me to assist you, to carry you, to feed you, and to be your son, again." Benedict sincerely said.

"Who are you? We don't need you here. Our son is already dead. He died when he did not choose us. He died when he preferred spending his whole life with the woman unworthy of appreciation and love. He died years ago." His mother furiously answered.

"Leave now. Go back to where you belong. You are just wasting your time." His father angrily added.

Upon hearing his parents' hurtful words, Benedict was weakened and decided to go back home. Sad it was, but again, he had to move on, even to the point of having no parents in his life and knowing the fact that they hated him. He narrated to Jade what happened and imprinted in his mind that his parents would no longer accept them. But since he is a loving and forgiving son, he did not hold grudges towards his parents, so Jade, who has been so loving to them since she was still young. They have placed their trust in the Lord that someday, Mr. and Mrs. Russelle would change their minds and have forgiving hearts.

One unexpected moment came that broke Deborah again into pieces. Benedict had severe disease. A disease they were not sure of the cure. They followed all the doctor's words and undertones of all medications, but Benedict was in serious pain. Days and months passed, Benedict's situation worsened. He could barely move. He could hardly breathe. On his death-bed, he slowly whispered these words to Jade:

"My love, this is the time that God has created for me. I am coming home. I am coming home to God's paradise. I might be leaving you physically, but know that in your heart, I am here. I am always here for you. Thank you for the memories we shared and the real love you let me experience. You made me the happiest man by letting me know you deeper and love you. Your heart is as pure as your parents. Despite being rejected by my father and mother, you never treated them as an enemy. Instead, you even valued them more." Benedict sadly expressed.

Jade did not say a word at all. She just kept on crying relentlessly while holding his husband's hands.

"Jade, promise me, take care of my parents while they are still alive. With that, I would be very happy." He requested.

"I will, my love. No matter how difficult it would be. No matter how many times they will push me away, again. I will. I will do this for you." She sorrowfully uttered.

Benedict passed away, Deborah mourned day and night. Despite the pain she is experiencing, she packed all her things and went to her in-law's house. She fulfilled her promise to Benedict.

"Mr. and Mrs. Russelle?" Deborah asked.

"What are you doing here?" Mrs. Russelle answered.

"I am here to offer myself in taking care of both of you. I am doing this for your son, Benedict, and for you, my second mother and father." She added.

"We do not need you here! We can handle ourselves. You better go and leave!" Mr. Russelle exclaimed.

In spite of all the hardships and cruelty they put her into, She did her very best to please the old and sick. She never complained and still served them patiently, hoping that God will continue to bless her every day, most especially now that she had no one else to talk and turn to, except God alone.

The story of Deborah is a resemblance to the story of Ruth, the Moabite. These two women are both examples of showing selfless love and intimacy to the world, just like our creator, despite having experienced difficult moments in life. Their faith was also shaken, but they remained faithful, trusting God's will and showed resilience, knowing that God is with them, in spirit and in truth.

God's fingerprints can be seen in Ruth's story. Ruth, after being widowed early in life, lived with her mother-in-law, took care of her, and followed God for all her days, believing he would provide for her. She had a long and challenging journey, but she received redemption from the Almighty Father. Ruth started her life empty, but she ended full, with God's grace.

The same way happened with Deborah. She showed love and intimacy to the people around her—Laura and Nelson, Mr. and

Mrs. Russelle, and Benedict. Ruth was an epitome of abiding loyalty and devotion. Tough situations like the unexpected death of her parents, rejection of Mr. & Mrs. Russelle, early passing of Benedict, and cruel experience while taking care of Benedict's parents led Deborah to be closer, more steadfast, and more zealous to God. Giving up never became her option. Instead, she faced every test bravely and allowed her unconditional love for them to prevail.

Ruth and Jade never felt any discouragement from their journey. These women are proof that God touched their lives in mysterious ways, knitted a fine-looking cross stitch, unfinished, but is in progress. He worked for the good of Ruth and Deborah, and for all women in the world.

Lord, my prayer remains the same, "Please, show me things for what they really are, that I might not be deceived and dishonor you."

STORY 4

UNDERSTAND WHO SHE IS

INTRODUCTION

Women are the solution to life problems and difficulties!

Keep an open mind and heart.

What I find truly remarkable; God has given me the subject woman to write about and gives me countless words scribing her. I want you to try and imagine this, God gives you the subject matter (woman) and tells you what to say; it's like I'm God puppet and Jesus Christ is pulling my strings to describe her! What do you do with that besides obey and be honored you were chosen. As I once said before, I'm not a scholar of writing, and I didn't do very well in school and in college in subjects, writing and English. But I was able to pass the classes because I had a teacher. Just as God is my teacher in writing about his subject (woman). I don't claim to know all about her. Only God knows that, but what I'm willing to share about her is given to me by TEACHER.

What you do not know you want to know, and once you do know, you will start to understand why she is unfinished. What you will come to know about her is only a small portion of what you don't. But in order? To get to know and understand her, and you still won't, until you believe God created her for us!

If you have read my book thus far, nothing tries to stop or start you from reading. It's just happened. Are you reading the book, or is the book reading you? It'd just happened like most things, and all things around you just happened. Is your heart beating, or you beat your heart? All just happened. I do believe she is God's solution for life and all humanity. She didn't just happen; she was created by the almighty God. The world turns, and you do nothing; it just happened.

The unfinished visibility of women is God's creation of the world, so his vision is clearly seen and understood. And one thing that is clearly made for humanity is her lifetime companionship.

Women's is the difference between words as art and words as stories; she is arguably the place where literature departs from print. I would argue God's unfinished Masterpiece is literature largely because her stories have significance only if you really like reading insightful novels—but If you are reading for the sake of reading, then it might be futile for you to get the message. Keep reading and learning God's choice would give you new perception, motivation, which makes you think about your choices and can change the way you look at life.

Reading has been a part of my life for more than half of my life, but reading took me on the journey to write about what I read. For me, every book changes me a bit. It exposes me to see how different people's minds work, how you can learn something from anyone without reading their work. I've learned that the world is not black and white but many shades of grey. Overall, it changed my life, and I am hoping that it would do the same for you and others.

No, that the wheels of readership grind slowly, and finally, in exasperation, I'll give you ownership of the manuscript and make it a daily read.

In the course of the years during which I have labored over for years writing this manuscript and others, I often made repeated changes here and there, and that will probably continue to be the case. But at some point, I must find the courage to let the manuscript leave my hand, even if I'm convinced there's much still need to be done.

The study of this iconic subject has been one of the artist or author world's most famous mysteries. While there are some, who claim "woman" is a thinly veiled portrait of the goddess who works is most commonly believed to be a cloth painting in motion. But there's no alternative title given to "woman" but God's Masterpiece of Creation and blessings to mankind."

Upon not completing the portrait, the artist sends it out to the world, where it ended up in everyone's collection. With many unanswered questions, like? How can I get my copy? Why is she so beautiful? How long will it take to complete her? Why is the Masterpiece of a woman? All these questions have long gone unanswered. And so, the mystery and unanswered questions will be answered, keep reading . . .

Think of it: being able to spend time in the presence of the Creator Unfinished Masterpiece Woman!

GOD left He unfinished so he can return and continue fine-tuning her, until one day she may be completely finished by Him. By chance, you don't understand that maybe because you're distracted by your ignorance. Even if you're reading my very interesting book, your mind may be somewhere else, but I'd suggest you read with a free mind, and you won't remember time passing as you read the book . . .

STORY #4: Understand who she is

My mind is never blank when I think of her; the more I think, the more I write about the endless subject matter of woman. But if I can't wake my fellow man up, I hope I can wake up other people who read this. You must train your mind; first, protect, blocked-out unimportant ideas to keep out negative energy about her energies.

A woman is a perfect blend of characters, which makes her somewhat impossible to comprehend her nature. With this, most men do not understand women. No wonder why they keep on searching, testing, and marrying as many women as they can. Even though they end up frustrated with their choices and even prefer their very first love, women evolve faster and become knowledgeable and wiser beyond the understanding of men. She easily captures man's thoughts and emotions in a single touch. Proverbs 7 warns sons against an adulterous woman. A man requires so much wisdom and insights to be able to escape the seductive words and actions of an adulterous woman. Such a woman is described as unruly and defiant. She applies charms that lead men astray. In the book of Judges, a man of strength and valor is conquered by Delilah . . .

A woman is a masterpiece that progresses with God's work of creation by exhibiting love, compassion, peace, and providence. Her brain is ingrained with a special intelligence that understands the surrounding and applies knowledge to bring solutions. A woman takes the role of an author or an artist that assembles skills and intuition to bring change in the society—a change brought by unwavering faith, coupled with good actions. For example, the Bible presents the life of Deborah. Deborah is one of the most influential women of the Bible. As a prophet, Judge Deborah was said to hear God's voice and share God's Word with others. As a priestess, she did not offer sacrifices, as the men did, but she did lead worship services and preached as a judge, was one of the rulers of the Hebrews and considered as the only female leader in the Old

Testament. She sought guidance from the Lord by praying and meditating before proclaiming their ruling on a matter.

Deborah would sit under the palm tree between Ramah and Bethel in the hill country of Ephraim, and the Israelites would line up for her to rule on a matter. As a warrior, Deborah, upon receiving instructions from God, called Barak, an Israelite warrior, to bring 10,000 troops up Mount Tabor to attack Sisera, Jabin's commander of troops. She willingly agreed to go to battle with Barak and the troops. Deborah and her story have lots of things to impart to us, like being obedient, being courageous, and being true to faith no matter what happens. She sincerely followed everything God commanded her to do, was bold enough to do something out of her comfort zone just to glorify Him, never wavered her faith despite all the struggles she faced, and always believed that God would faithfully guide her and lead her to the right path. Just like her, Aliyah is another woman who is a perfect representation of how faith works in her life.

This is her story . . .

To bring difference was her greatest dream, and to bring hope was her ultimate mission.

In a town where poor people really have to grind hard in order to bring food on the table, release blood and sweat in order to sustain their needs, and sacrifice everything just to make every waking day a lighter one for their loved ones, most especially to their children; there is this young girl named Aliyah, full of faith, that one day, her little and simple actions would cause transformation in the way people live and think in their place.

With her innocent mind and young age, her parents have already seen her as a goal-driven daughter. In everything that she does, she always makes sure she has given her best. She had displayed so much excellence, especially in terms of academics. Aliyah never considered their situation, being poor, as a hindrance to her studies. She was also blessed because her parents were very supportive and loving.

One fine morning, she approached her parents on the farm.

"Mom, Pa. You need not work like this when I become a professional. I promise to give you a good life. I will build you a safe home, provide you delicious foods we have never tasted, bring you to places we have never been, and we will together help more those who are in need of us."

"Your dreams are as wide as this farm, Aliyah. Like the farm, a rough soil, while there is smooth. But despite that, we really know you can do it. Just put your trust in the Lord. Nothing is impossible with Him. But also, you need to work hard for your dreams. We are with you, Aliyah, no matter what happens." Her parents responded.

"I also want to become a teacher, Ma, and Pa. I want my students to see hope in me and consider my own personal life as a motivation and example for them to also chase their dreams, no matter how difficult life would be." She added.

"We are very sure you will become what you want because you have a pure heart, and your faith in God is big, my daughter." Her father replied.

Not all the kids in the town, so as their parents, considered education as an important tool for success and bringing change. Others believed their children would still end up digging into the farm and fishing in the river, just like them, while some found it impossible to finish because of scarcity. On the other hand, Aliyah's parents were not like them. They valued education. They did not want their daughter to turn out to be like them: have not finished schooling, were not able to land a decent job, and had difficulty in providing for their needs. This was the very reason why they walked with Aliyah all the way in reaching her dreams.

During her elementary and secondary years, she showed extraordinary potential. Every exam she took was just like a piece of cake. She always got a perfect score, even in performances. She was also called as the great mathematician by her classmates and friends, for she could do mental calculations. All her teachers liked her, for aside from being smart, she has a pleasing attitude. Her image was very respectable.

On her graduation day in high school, her parents burst into tears, most especially when people applauded and cheered when Aliyah's name was called as a valedictorian. She received 20 different medals in total for all her special awards and clubs and organizations joined at.

"We are just so glad to witness this milestone of yours, Aliyah. We have made it here. We will still make it to the next level, which is your college journey. We will always be here for you, our daughter. You have made us proud all the time." Her parents expressed.

"All of these are for you and for the Lord, Ma... Pa... Thank you so much for everything that you did just to support my studies. It must have been very hard for both of you, but you still opted to work day and night just for me to be closer to my dreams. You are my inspiration." Aliyah responded.

Aliyah's parents looked for ways in order to send her to a prestigious university in the United States. Even if they will be far from each other, the parents just considered it to be a beautiful sacrifice, for in exchange would be their daughter's dreams and goals in life. Because of Aliyah's extraordinary intelligence, she was granted a full scholarship at Princeton University—a well-known school for highly-intellectual and gifted students. Out of the many courses offered in the university, she chose a degree in Elementary Education.

Years had passed; she graduated from college. She made her parents happier and prouder. Aliyah immediately took the board exam and became a Licensed Teacher. Everyone was in awe of her achievements.

"My daughter, what are your plans now?" Her mother asked.

"Ma, I would like to teach the children at Pag-asa (another term for hope)." She replied.

"Pag-asa? Are you sure? Why there? That is so far from here, and you know very well that the town has lots of rebels and criminals. What if you get hurt?" Her father added.

"My daughter, why not work in the US, instead. You will be safer there, and more opportunities will knock into your doors. Many universities would be fighting, just to have you." Her mother exclaimed.

"But . . . Ma . . . Pa . . . this was my childhood dream. Could you still remember the time I told you I want every child to see hope in me through my actions? This is now my chance to do it, and I want to pursue my dream in Pag-asa. I won't get harmed. I promise I will take care of myself. Let us just continue trusting the Lord. He will always protect me there and you here in our town." Aliyah convincedly said to her parents.

Her parents allowed her to do what she really wanted. Aliyah applied in Pag-asa and got hired right away. Aside from the fact that she was more than qualified, no other applicant risked applying in the said town for its highly known bad image. Days passed, Aliyah started to teach in Pag-Asa, and joyfully enjoyed her profession. All the children in the school loved her, for they have seen hope in her. Her words and actions were very influential, and they were touched with Aliyah's story in reaching her dreams. They even wished to be like Aliyah someday. Aliyah also made the children believe that no matter how chaotic their town would be, there will come a time that everything will change because every single person in that place will bring a difference.

One bright sunny afternoon, while Aliyah and her pupils had a simultaneous reading activity, a number of armed men entered their school. Upon seeing it, Aliyah placed the children into a safer area in the classroom and instructed them not to panic and do all that she says!

"Please do follow every word that I say, okay? By the time a rebel will enter the room, a person whom you can see, bringing a gun, all of you must be very quick in moving. You have to escape one by one, but kindly make sure the rebel could not sense at all what you are doing. Do not be afraid, my dear pupils; we can get through this. Trust in the Lord, Your God. He will protect us."

The children clearly understood their plan but were honestly shaking inside because of fear. One rebel, loaded with guns, entered the room to look for a possible child hostage whom they can use to get their demands from the government. Aliyah bravely approached the rebel and fearlessly attacked him until all the children were able to go out. Nonetheless, as the very last student was able to escape, the armed man pulled the trigger of his gun towards Aliyah.

The rebels moved rapidly and left the school, upon hearing the sound of the police car. That signaled them that policemen were coming. The cops checked all the classrooms and found out Aliyah's body lying on the floor, surrounded with blood.

"Teacher Aliyah, wake up! Please wake up. You are not dead. Wake up now." The pupil's weepily said.

The children mourned for Aliyah's death. People who knew her were saddened about what happened. Above all, her parents were grieving of the short-lived life of their daughter. They were in great sorrow.

"You do not deserve this, my daughter. All you wish is to touch other's lives by spreading hope to their eyes and faith in their hearts. I already warned you not to teach in Pag-Asa, but you insisted. We allowed you to do your chosen path, for we know that everything that you willingly does makes you truly happy, but this is not the destiny I prayed for you." Aliya's mother expressed while crying.

"Rest in peace now, my sweet, caring, and loving Aliyah. Your death really saddened us and broke our hearts. We could no longer feel your embrace, see your cheerful face, and feel your charming presence. In spite of what happened to you, we are somewhat at peace since we know that you are in better hands. You are now with our creator. Your heroic act and the good life you lived will always be remembered by us and by the people in our place. You have always made us proud. Until we meet again, our daughter. We love you very much." Her father sorrowfully added.

Aliyah's life continued to inspire all the people in the village. She dedicated and sacrificed her very self just for others to live. She may have died, but the way she lived her life with hope and the change she brought to her place lasted forever, in all generations that come.

The story of Aliyah is like the story of Deborah. As the only female judge mentioned in the Bible, Deborah is known for being a compassionate leader, just like Aliyah. She excelled in multiple areas. Clearly, one of the Bible's most outstanding figures, she served ancient Israel as a prophet, judge, military leader, songwriter, and a minstrel (Judges 4-5). The two chapters show her exemplary moral character and indicate the people gave her great love and respect. Like Moses before and David afterward, Deborah fused in herself the roles of prophet, national leader, and military commander. She led Israel for 60 years in the 12th century B.C. She proves that leadership resides not in gender but in character and gifting. The Israelites recognized her abilities and prospered under her tenure. Deborah means bee or even honeybee.

Aliyah, on the other hand, lived a good and inspiring life since she was still young. She was into loving and obeying her parents, helping others, working hard in order to reach her parents' and her own personal dreams, and above all, inspiring others through her actions and words. Years passed, Aliyah was able to do what she wanted.

Taught in a school where danger is very prone in the area, led the pupils in the place, but still ended up being killed by a rebel knowing that she secured and saved first the lives of her pupils over her own. In spite of the sad ending she got, when she was still alive, she was able to touch other's lives and inspire others to dream bigger since hope is always present, no matter what hurdles tried to shake her.

Most significantly, her faith in God never changed, and she just surrendered everything to Him. Aliyah might have lived a short life, but the change she brought to every heart and mind of the people of Pag-asa and her entire town is irreplaceable and very precious.

The stories of Deborah and Aliyah are powerful examples of how faith in action works. The story is an influential epitome of God's unfinished nature of showing compassion ingrained in women.

PS: One woman's dreams shattered by evildoers, in my opinion, the schools haven't taken the Lord's prayer and the Pledged to the Alligiance to the flag. The students need something to bring them together, which is much bigger than themselves. But we're too worried about trying to be politically correct that we are losing sight of what is important for our children, and that is the love of God and country. All schools should begin their day with love and unity; this will push out evil ideas and thoughts

STORY 5

CO-CREATOR

INTRODUCTION

God the decider, yet left her undone:
The story shows it just the way some men think and try to bankrupt God's grace, whome tries to sucked the life out of her. But his indebtedness paid for something very remarkable. The notion of womanhood as dependency on a man is absurd for her eyes are symbolically equated to the opened window with a "double vision." Her entire being is joined with all the secret power implies she is a (VIRTUOUS WOMAN) woman, in her sacred place.

Her positions will naturally emerge in an effort to establish a balanced dialogue between men and women living in this world. A place that humans inhabit becomes sacredly in a place and time for worship.

My dear readers, before you go any further, you need to know something about me. I say what I mean and mean what I'm saying, in all of my books and in life. If you don't want to know the truth, then don't ask me . I'm not afraid to stand firm with my elbows out on any of the Wordsworth decisions I made in writing any of my books. Too get your attention and trust for you to believe instinctively as you read.

On this day as you start reading my book, opened, your hearts and minds to the unique gift given to me by Jesus Christ to give to the people. As I mentioned before I'm not an educated literature scholarship author, I'm just a man using his God given gift. It'd give me honour to experience and express why I was chosen, but I'm joyful in the experience of God's will.

People all over the world depend on religion and women to create order in an otherwise unorganized university of humanity. Philosophical thought is utilized rationally to imagine a world where things happen for a reason.

STORY #5: Co-creator

GOD IS THE AUTHOR of all human life. Human life is sacred because, from the very beginning, it clearly involves the creative action of God, and it remains forever in a special relationship with the Creator, who is its sole end. God alone is the Lord of life from its beginning until its end: no one can under any circumstance claim for himself the right directly to destroy an innocent human being.

Through co-creation, salvation is brought to the world. A woman is considered a co-creator with God. She continues God's work of creation by giving birth. The story explains the nature of women in giving birth and taking care of children. Virtues and attributes upon which perfection and exaltation depend come naturally to a woman and are refined through marriage and motherhood. More description is given on the purpose of the female gender and why it was important. The co-creator nature of women is equivalent to the role played by Mary, the mother of Jesus, and Elizabeth, her cousin. Also, the story examines the story of Sara and her role in bringing forth a blessed generation.

Mary is one of the most admired and appreciated biblical figures. Her willingness to be a vessel for God's Messiah is inspirational, especially when you consider the confusion associated with a young, unmarried woman showing up pregnant—and the pain of watching your grown child be tried and crucified. Mary played a prominent role as the mother of Jesus Christ. Her love and care for her son, the son of God, can serve as a great example for mothers today. Mary demonstrated the power of pure faith. When you look at her accomplishments, it might not seem like she did very much. But her obedience changed the course of history. Sometimes the most profound thing we can do with our lives is to wholeheartedly say, "I am the Lord's servant."

Elizabeth, on the other hand, is righteous and blameless. She observed all the Lord's commands and decreed blamelessly. She was described as barren, unable to have children. In the bible, she is said to be an old woman. Regardless of how old she actually was, she was certainly past anyone would consider child-bearing age. But everything changed because of a miracle. She and her husband Zechariah was given a child named John. Their sincere and long-lasting faith in the Lord allowed them to be given the gift they were asking and longing for.

Sarah, Abraham's wife, is also a co-creator in the bible. When God instructed Abraham to leave his home for a land that God had in mind for him and his family and was promised that He would make him a great nation and bless him, Sarah supported her because of their great faith in the Lord. One thing they asked hard to the Lord is for them to be given a child. And by faith, even Sarah, who was also past childbearing age, was entitled to bear children because she considered Him faithful who had made the promise.

Just like Mary, Elizabeth, and Sarah, the life story of Caroline is another perfect example of co-creation.

This is her story . . .

In a far-flung region in Utah, there lived happily a very simple, beautiful, hardworking, and God-fearing woman named Caroline. She was appreciated and adored by many because of her goodness. But of all the men who tried to woo her, only this man with integrity, self-confidence, optimism, positive attitude, and great faith in the Lord, made it. This lad was christened as Rafael. He made Caroline the apple of his eyes. And so, the time came they realized that they were not only meant to just be together, but to spend the rest of their lives with each other, forever. They decided to get married and had high hopes that God would bless their marriage and plans. Caroline and Rafael have been wedded for 20 years already. The love and care they have for each other never changed. However, something lacked, and that is, they never had a child. Having one was their utmost longing as a couple. They genuinely prayed to the Almighty Father and willingly visited all churches around the world just to show God how heartfelt they were in their desire. All their concerned relatives told them to just adopt a child in order to fill in the missing piece they experienced, but their faith never wavered. The couple never missed pleading for what they ask for, not even a single minute, not a single moment.

On the day of their 21st wedding anniversary, a very wonderful and sought-after miracle happened. Caroline got pregnant. The time she knew it, she immediately thanked the Lord for making her dream a reality. Filled with excitement, she ran into her husband, who was taking care of their animals, and happily shared with him their answered prayer. Rafael's expressions upon hearing the shocking news were incomparable and indescribable. They delighted and called for a feast, together with their families. The best foods and drinks were served. The finest music was also heard.

"My husband! My husband! Come here! I could not believe that after two decades, God finally answered our prayer. I am pregnant. I'm pregnant! This is by far the greatest gift we have received from Him. Thank you very much, Our Saviour." Caroline uttered.

"Hoooh! Thank you, Lord. Thank you so much for this gift. My wife, He deserves more of us. We have to praise and serve Him more for what He gave us. We are more than blessed to finally have a child. How could we repay God, Caroline? He is so good." Rafael responded.

"We will raise this gift according to His words and will. This child will also serve God undoubtedly, just like us." The wife added.

"I will take good care of you and my child, as much as I can, until my last breath." The Husband promised.

During her pregnancy, Caroline was well taken care of by her husband and all the people who love and care for them. As an ideal husband, Rafael never failed to make sure that she had everything she needed and wanted. All her food cravings were provided and fulfilled. Nourishing meals and boundless assistance from her husband were also given.

Finally! Caroline gave birth. She successfully delivered a baby boy. Their baby's first cry brought them into tears, and thanked the Lord again for a wonderful and priceless blessing.

"He has your eyes and lips, my husband." Caroline tearfully said.

"He has your good heart, my wife. I love you both." Rafael happily answered.

They named their baby, Nathan, which means "God's gift." They purposely chose that name to honor the giver of their son's life. Nathan grew up to be a healthy baby boy. As years passed by, just like his parents, Nathan became very religious. He was also cheerful, friendly, hardworking, and loving. Rafael and Caroline reared Nathan well, knowing how to respect others older than him or anyone who is in authority. They know they have not failed as parents. However, everything started to change on his 15th birthday. He was diagnosed with Leukemia. Caroline and Rafael were both saddened. They were shocked and could not accept that God gave them a baby for a short period of time but will be taken away from them.

In all means, they did everything that they could in order to help Nathan heal. They worked tirelessly, day and night, to be able to pay for all the pricey medicines. Because of over fatigue and exhaustion, Rafael unexpectedly died. Caroline felt broken. The entire burden was left to her, and she started losing her faith. Her trust in God was shaken. She blamed Him now for everything that happened to her family, saying that He might be playing some sort of cosmic joke on her family.

"Why on earth did this happen to me? Of all the people in the world, why my loved ones? First, my only son who is very ill. Now, my loving husband. I lost the love of my life. I lost my partner, the one who always told me that you were just trying to test our faith. Is this still a test? We trusted you. We worshipped you. We served you. My husband is gone! What have we done to you? What have we missed? Did I fail in my faith? Did I ever forget you? Answer me!!! Answer me please!!!" Caroline angrily shouted while facing the heavens.

With this, she started to avoid the church for a very long time. Praying and worshipping were also neglected. Meanwhile, Nathan's illness became more critical. Complications arose. The doctor firmly believed and said he had only six months left to live.

Caroline felt downhearted. The situation seemed to be so heavy and unbearable. After talking with the doctor, she passed by a church, for she realized something important. She grasped it was high time to pass all her problems and surrender all her worries to the Lord. She badly needed Him, His guidance, and His comfort. As she entered the church, she knelt down and prayed while crying. She blubbered rivers of tears in front of the altar and asked for forgiveness. She asked the Lord to take her son's illness. She promised that she and her son would render their lives for the greater glory of God. She submitted everything to the Lord and allowed Him to take control of their lives.

"Heavenly Father, pardon me for blaming you, for questioning you, for doubting you, and for unloving you. I regretted everything that I did. I was truly reminded of my husband's words. He once told me that no matter how zigzag and hopeless life would be, one person I should not hate about and should always seek is You, for you are our Alpha and our Omega. Forgive me, my Lord. Please absolve my trespasses. I know you have better plans for us and valid reasons why such things occurred. One last thing I would like to ask you is my son's healing. Grant my prayer, Oh God. Listen to my heart's plea. I will do all things for You, just like what we used to do before. In Jesus Name, Amen." Caroline genuinely said.

The following week, after their check-up with the Doctor, another unexpected miracle happened. People were truly shocked. Even the doctors were so clueless and admitted that it was indeed a miracle. Leukemia is now gone.

"This is impossible. Look, the results show that Nathan is now free of Leukemia. He is totally healed. I could not explain the reason why this happened. Even other doctors, for sure, could not justify this scenario. This must have been a miracle!" Nathan's doctor amazingly expressed.

Everyone was so glad, most especially Caroline. True to her words, they attended church again. Nathan decided to enter the priesthood. He wished to know God better and considered his second life a way to serve Him for the rest of his life. Caroline wanted to say no, for she will be left all alone. But then, she reh'hu'9' membered her sincere promise to the Lord. Nathan belonged to God. She allowed him to do what he wanted. Years had passed, and so Nathan became a priest. During Nathan's very first homily, Caroline died in her sleep, at peace, knowing that she was coming home to the Lord's kingdom. Nathan felt down upon hearing the news but was able to heartily accept it because of his faith in God. He knew his mother is in a happy place where she was destined to be.

Mary's and Elizabeth's Faith

. . . God sent the angel Gabriel to Nazareth, a city in Galilee, to a virgin who was engaged to a man named Joseph, a descendant of David's house. The virgin's name was Mary . . . The angel said, "Don't be afraid, Mary. God is honoring you. Look! You will conceive and give birth to a son, and you will name him Jesus. He will be great, and he will be called the Son of the Highest. Luke 1:26-27, 30-32 CEB

When Gabriel visits Mary a few months later, she also asks a question in response to the amazing message she receives. Her question, however, did not come from disbelief. She asks, "How will this happen since I haven't had sexual relations with a man?" It is often noted that Zechariah—an elderly and experienced priest serving in the temple in Jerusalem—doubted the angel, while Mary—a teenager living in a village in Galilee—responded in faith. Mary obediently accepted the astonishing news the angel brought her and replied, "I am the Lord's servant. Let it be with me just as you have said" (Luke 1:38).

Zechariah's doubt also contrasts with his wife's faith. Elizabeth's faith is remarkable, considering she probably received the news about her pregnancy second-hand through her now mute husband. "In contrast to her husband, there is no narrative indication of unbelief or surprise on her behalf, only a response of praise for her having conceived." (p. 39) Furthermore, just as her infertility and late pregnancy echo the experiences of several prominent Old Testament women, so does her expression of thanks offered to God: "This is the Lord's doing. He has shown his favor to me by removing my disgrace among other people" (Luke 1:25; cf. Rachel in Gen. 30:23).

The story of Caroline is like the story of Mary, mother of Jesus, and Elizabeth, her cousin. They are both examples of unwavering faith. Mary was very young when the angel appeared before her to tell her that she will bear a child. Although Mary knows the consequences of having a child without the sanctity of marriage, she trusted the Lord.

Like Mary, Caroline trusted that the Lord would hear her prayers. She never felt hopeless despite the many years that passed without having a child. She did everything she could just for God to grant her request. And so, she was given what she wanted. Her family thought everything was already stable and fine, but two tragic things happened—his son's illness and his husband's death. In spite of these challenges, including the times she lost faith in Him, she bowed down, asking for forgiveness and offered herself back to the Lord. She devoted all her life to Jesus and loving her only son as much as she could. Even when the time came that her son asked her permission to enter the priesthood, her loving nature as a mother prevailed. Caroline allowed her son to do what he wanted, even if, in return, she lived alone. She just really let the Lord take control over her life and dedicated her whole life in order to glorify him.

These women lived the words from Luke 1:45, which says, "Blessed is she who has believed that the Lord would fulfill His promises to her!"

STORY 6

REPENTANT SINNER

INTRODUCTION

Time in her time has time for us.

There are discrepancies and contradictions here and there about her and her responsibility because her histories are written through the eyes and cultural lenses of different men with variations.

The History of Middle-earth has some very old versions of the story about her, and I only feel sorry for them. Let me explain something she was hardly mentioned in later writings due to the fact she is superior and was intentionally left out. Some may be unhappy with my explanation, as I explain in the stories and other notes. So, I explained all of the possible origins and arguments against anyone who just states as a matter of fact from his point of view she is not?

It's all part of her creation for me, and I am uninterested if someone says, "but that's not true," well . . . ok then, but you're missing out on a lot of what God's promise. I draw the line at writing outside of my spirituality knowledge about her. This may lead me to be vulnerable to interpretations by other people. I will say, though, that my own view on this issue is just that, my own. While I think it's wrong to disregard a lot of what I should not stop you from formulating your own answers here.

If your answers are different, "maybe I don't know, nothing of this," then I am free to write my own answer quoting from my sources. It is then up to the readers to regard or disregard anything they like or doesn't like. It's exactly what I do with all the information in the books, regard it or disregard based on your own opinions what I consider valid. Just don't comment saying I'm wrong to write about her, please!

As I'm closing this story, it's maybe impossible to determine absolutely what is correct or not. With the big issues the author mentions, I tend to give all versions of the storylines, and it doesn't really bother me that you don't have a definitive answer, because any of them could be true, or parts of all answered could be truthful. It's left up to you.

A small analogy When you love someone very much, and they die, do you simply throw out their clothes, or do you bury your nose deep inside them? Do you simply ignore the last vestiges of the beauty they offered you? No, you keep it! So you the reader's keep inserting and adding yourself in the book as you read, therefore readers by adding yourself to the book stories the book will never be finished like women will never be finished until God finished her!

"Life is static."

STORY #6: Repentant sinner

ALL WOMEN, SINCE EVE, the world's first sinner, were born in sin, and sinners by birth became more or fewer sinners by practice. Despite this, God forgives every single person. He forgives women.

In Luke 7:48-50, it says that Jesus is not excusing immorality. Rather, he is manifesting a compassionate understanding of people who commit serious sins but who then show that they are sorry and turn to Christ for relief. And what relief this woman feels when Jesus says: "Your sins are forgiven . . . Your faith has saved you; go in peace." Mary Magdalene's life is a strong example of a woman being a repentant sinner. In the bible, Mary Magdalene was identified with the city woman who was a sinner. That woman, who had many sins, bathed Jesus' feet with her tears, wiped his feet with her hair, and anointed his feet with oil. The seven demons cast out of Mary Magdalene were identified with seven deadly sins. One of those sins was lust. Jesus told the chief priests and elders of his people that tax collectors and prostitutes were entering the Kingdom of God ahead of them.

Mary Magdalene was the first person to see the resurrected Jesus. She was thus identified as a repentant prostitute. Identifying Mary Magdalene as a prostitute tends to separate her from men. Relative to women, men historically have lacked equal opportunity to become prostitutes. In the Christian bible, Jesus told the chief priests and elders of his people that tax collectors and prostitutes were entering the Kingdom of God ahead of them. Mary Magdalene could have been identified as a tax collector or some other type of bureaucrat. Thinking of Mary Magdalene as a bureaucrat would help men to identify with her and to recognize that they, too, could be privileged in entering the Kingdom of God.

Mary's desperate longing to be close to Christ, to serve Him in any way she could, became the way she lived her life. She knew she would not have a life to live if not for Him. What Mary lived daily is the faith we all strive to achieve. Just like Mary Magdalene, the life of Annabelle manifests a life of a repentant sinner.

This is her story . . .

Think of the most expensive branded clothing, the latest in-demand gadget, the best gold and diamond accessories, and the greatest luxurious sports car. Name them; she has it all.

Arrogant, spoiled, bossy, insensitive, mean, rude, wild. These undesirable and not-so-good-to-hear qualities of a lady, describe her as a whole.

Being born and raised in a very wealthy and famous family, Annabelle experienced all the lavish things and privileges she wished and wanted. Her parents gave her everything and treated her like a princess in all Disney movies. All the comfort life has to offer was enjoyed and adored by her. However, she lived her life without a sense of purpose. In fact, her daily route only grasped various malls and night bars. She also engaged herself in illegal drugs and alcoholic drinking. Annabelle embraced the term YOLO—You Only Live Once.

"Come on, guys! Have fun. The night is still young! Loosen up—dance like crazy. Drinks are unlimited. Just order anything. I'll pay for it. Have fun, guys! Hoooh! This is the best night ever!" Annabelle excitedly shouted while loud, upbeat music was played.

"Hey, Annabelle! Are you OK? You seem so tipsy already. I think you should go home now. Take a rest. Your parents will surely get worried about you." A friend asked.

"Since when did you care? And for your information, my parents won't get mad at me. They love me. By the way, what do you think of me? Loser? I can handle myself well, I guess you should be the one going home." She stutteringly responded.

A few minutes later, while everyone's happily dancing and drinking, Annabelle's friends were shocked when she unexpectedly passed out. One of them hurriedly called her bodyguard and took her home.

"Look at our daughter. Are we wrong in raising her? It really pains me to see her like this. We have given our best for her." Annabelle's mom sadly expressed.

"We did everything we could, my wife. We worked hard just to give her the life we have not experienced before. I hope she'll change. I just really hope she will." Her father added.

The morning came. In the house, while the whole family is eating breakfast, Annabelle's mom received a phone call from the university in which her daughter is enrolled. It is already the principal who had informed them of Annabelle's performance in school. Only at that very moment, they knew their daughter's real situation.

Annabelle skipped classes for quite a time already, for she thought she no longer needed a college diploma and a degree. After all, from her own perspective, she will still end up working in her own company. She knew their family had lots of money to finance her in all aspects of life.

"I do apologize for my daughter's lapses, Mrs. Bill. I will work on this. Again, on behalf of our family, I am deeply sorry. Thank you so much for the concern. "Annabelle's mom said.

Upon hearing the words of her mom, Annabelle anxiously and hurriedly stood and said I'm going back to my room for some important stuff, but her mom stopped her.

"Where do you think you are going? What have you done, Annabelle? We gave everything you wanted. Whatever you asked, we immediately provided it with just a snap of a finger. Your dad and I worked hard for you. We sent you to the most exclusive and costly top-performing university for you to at least finish a degree and receive a diploma. You wasted that chance. Your allowance was more than enough. We even bought your cars every year, hired three maids just to attend to your needs and wants, chose competent and skilled drivers who could also protect you from any harm. You could even shop all day and night. What else could you ask for?" Her Mom angrily complained.

Annabelle just smiled and acted like she did not hear a word.

"Look at you! Is that what you dreamed of looking at and becoming? We've already given you countless chances, but you misused them. Painful, it may be to us, but we have to do this. We have decided. From now on, you no longer belong to this family. Seek help from your friends for they're more important to you. Pack your things, N-O-W!" His Dad sadly expressed with conviction.

Her parents intentionally did it to teach her a lesson. They said Annabelle could only expect support from them until she learns a lesson out of her own doings. Because of what happened, she lost all she has—money, cars, maids, and drivers. She became homeless. Money had become one of his major problems, as well. In this dark time of her life, no single friend ever helped her.

"How dare you do this to me? You adored my company before. Now that I needed you most, all of you seemed to be invisible.

Annabelle's life became darker. She continued drinking and taking illegal drugs. In order to support her vices, she became a drug pusher.

"Amazing! This is easy money. I love this!" She said.

One Saturday evening, she was secretly selling drugs in a distant area but did not know that the buyer was a policeman. He was caught and brought directly to prison. Hoping that her parents would bring her out, she tried calling them many times, but she received no response. She remembered her parents saying they will not help her in any means unless she changes for the better. Annabelle felt hopeless and depressed.

Limited food to eat; limited water to drink; and limited space to rest. These were the challenges she faced inside the jail. It was the kind of life she hadn't faced before when she was still under her parents' care. The added problem is dangerous and unruly inmates who have committed heinous crimes. She did not have any person to talk to, but there's this black woman with a motherly figure who kept on looking at her.

"Hi, young lady. I am Nahla. How about you? What should I call you?" The black woman asked.

Instead of answering, Annabelle remained silent while looking at her.

"Don't be afraid of me. I won't hurt you. I can be a friend." She added.

"I am Annabelle," Annabelle answered shortly.

From that moment, they started talking frequently. Annabelle felt comfortable with Nahla. She had that inexpressible motherly care. Nahla, in return, took care of Annabelle and treated her like her own daughter. They both shared each other's personal stories and reasons why they committed such crimes. Most significantly, Nahla led her to the right path, the path to Jesus. She always encouraged Annabelle to attend Bible study with her. Annabelle looked back at her past practices and realized something.

"My parents' efforts became fruitless due to the choices I have made in the past. So much time was lost, but I believe it is never too late to change. Jesus, I wished I have known you earlier. I wished I had not hurt my parents. I wished I had not used all the money I had in helping others. I wished I had not abused myself by using illegal drugs and excessive alcohol drinking. Thank you, Lord, for using Nahla as an instrument in drawing me closer to you. I regretted everything I did before. Forgive me, father. I promise to change myself, especially when I get the chance to come out of prison." Annabelle sincerely whispered to God while crying.

Nahla's time served in prison is up and she, finally getting out of prison. She promised Annabelle that once she gets out, her home is open for her.

"Thank you, Annabelle, for the care and love you showed me. Never thought you would totally change yourself for good. We should always rejoice in the Lord, for he touched your heart and made it pure. See you when I see you." Nahla uttered.

"How could I repay your goodness, Nahla? You have led me to the path I was never into. A million thanks for the friendship and motherly love. Please continue to pray for me. I will be missing you here. God bless on your new journey." Annabelle replied.

Months passed, and Annabelle was freed from prison. She instantly looked for Nahla, and she was welcomed by her with open arms. She kept her promise of living a different life. She started doing purposeful activities such as volunteering for orphanages and homes for the aged on weekdays. She embraced the church on weekends and always attended Sunday worship.

When her parents knew and saw that she had changed, she was welcomed back to the family.

"Mom and Dad, I thank you for the discipline you instilled in me. Without you disowning me before, maybe I am still in night bars until now, doing undesirable things. Thank you for not giving up on me. You have truly waited for my coming." Annabelle conveyed.

Annabelle is now using her second chance and blessed life to help those who have fewer in life. She donated to charities and did volunteer work together with Nahla. Her parents also showed full support for the new journey taken by their daughter.

The story of Annabelle is like the story of Mary Magdalene. Mary Magdalene was a figure in the Bible's New Testament who was one of Jesus' most loyal followers and is said to have been the first to witness his resurrection. She is described as a repentant sinner, just like Annabelle in this story.

From the New Testament, one can conclude that Mary of Magdala, her hometown, a village on the shore of the Sea of Galilee, was a leading figure among those attracted to Jesus. When the men in that company abandoned him at the hour of mortal danger, Mary of Magdala was one of the women who stayed with him, even to the Crucifixion. She was present at the tomb, the first person to whom Jesus appeared after his resurrection and the first to preach the "Good News" of that miracle. These are among the few specific assertions made about Mary Magdalene in the Gospels.

In Eastern Christian tradition, <u>Mary Magdalene</u> is regarded as having lived a life of great virtue. She is regarded as having been a close companion of Mary, the mother of Jesus. In western Christian tradition, various Mary's within the Gospels were identified with Mary Magdalene. Mary Magdalene came to be regarded as a repentant prostitute only in the western Christian tradition.

Annabelle, on the other hand, lived a luxurious life but without having a sense of purpose. Instead of using her money and privileges in good ways, just like helping others, she chose a different kind of path. A track where all undesirable things are included and embraced. With this, she was taught a lesson from his parents, which caused her to live a very meek life, so far from what she was used to having. Annabelle continued her chosen life and indulged herself in alcoholic drinking and illegal drugs. With this, she was put to prison due to a terrible crime—a type of situation she never thought she could experience. She has lived a very hard life, which is typical for incarcerated people but is always deeply upsetting. She felt like she was abandoned by everybody, most especially her parents. But everything changed when she met this woman named Nahla. This lass introduced Annabelle to the words of God and led her close to Him—a feeling and connection she did not experience in the past. Right there and then, she realized something. She realized that everything she did before was not just a waste of time, but also a waste of relationship with her parents and with God.

Nahla somewhat became Annabelle's angel, an instrument purposely given by God from above. Annabelle was given another fulfilling life to live. A second chance, so to speak. So she went back to her parents and asked for forgiveness. Her parents accepted her fully, just as how God acknowledged her. Annabelle truly became a repentant sinner. She believed in 2 Chronicles 7:14/ NIV, which says, "If my people, who are called by my name, will humble themselves and pray and seek my face and turn from their wicked ways, then I will hear from heaven, and I will forgive their sin and will heal their land."

The life of both Mary Magdalene and Annabelle taught us to repent our sins to God and that there is always a second chance for those who truly believe in Him. "Repent, then, and turn to God so that your sins may be wiped out, that times of refreshing may come from the Lord."—**Acts 3:19/ NIV**

STORY 7

WOMAN COURAGEOUS AND FEARLESS

INTRODUCTION

http://www.gutenberg.org/files/8710/8710-h/8710-h.htm

Judges 4 New International Version (NIV)

Deborah

4 Again the Israelites did evil in the eyes of the Lord, now that Ehud was dead. 2 So the Lord sold them into the hands of Jabin king of Canaan, who reigned in Hazor. Sisera, the commander of his army, was based in Harosheth Haggoyim. 3 Because he had nine hundred chariots fitted with iron and had cruelly oppressed the Israelites for twenty years, they cried to the Lord for help.

5 Now Deborah, a prophet, the wife of Lappidoth, was leading[a] Israel at that time. 5 She held court under the Palm of Deborah between Ramah and Bethel in the hill country of Ephraim, and the Israelites went up to her to have their disputes decided. 6 She sent for Barak son of Abinoam from Kedesh in Naphtali and said to him, "The Lord, the God of Israel, commands you: 'Go, take with you ten thousand men of Naphtali and Zebulun and lead them up to Mount Tabor. 7 I will lead Sisera, the commander of Jabin's army, with his chariots and his troops to the Kishon River and give him into your hands.'"

8 Barak said to her, "If you go with me, I will go; but if you don't go with me, I won't go."

9 "Certainly, I will go with you," said Deborah. "But because of the course you are taking, the honor will not be yours, for the Lord will deliver Sisera into the hands of a woman." So Deborah went with Barak to Kedesh. 10 There, Barak summoned Zebulun and Naphtali, and ten thousand men went up under his command. Deborah also went up with him.

11 Now Heber the Kenite had left the other Kenites, the descendants of Hobab, Moses' brother-in-law,[b] and pitched his tent by the great tree in Zaanannim near Kedesh.

12 When they told Sisera that Barak son of Abinoam had gone up to Mount Tabor, 13 Sisera summoned from Harosheth Haggoyim to the Kishon River all his men and his nine hundred chariots fitted with iron.

14 Then Deborah said to Barak, "Go! This is the day the Lord has given Sisera into your hands. Has not the Lord gone ahead of you?" So Barak went down Mount Tabor, with ten thousand men following him. 15 At Barak's advance, the Lord routed Sisera and all his chariots and army by the sword, and Sisera got down from his chariot and fled on foot.

16 Barak pursued the chariots and army as far as Harosheth Haggoyim, and all Sisera's troops fell by the sword; not a man was left. 17 Sisera, meanwhile, fled on foot to the tent of Jael, the wife of Heber the Kenite, because there was an alliance between Jabin king of Hazor, and the family of Heber the Kenite.

18 Jael went out to meet Sisera and said to him, "Come, my lord, come right in. Don't be afraid." So he entered her tent, and she covered him with a blanket.

19 "I'm thirsty," he said. "Please give me some water." She opened a skin of milk, gave him a drink, and covered him up.

20 "Stand in the doorway of the tent," he told her. "If someone comes by and asks you, 'Is anyone in there?' say 'No.'"

21 But Jael, Heber's wife, picked up a tent peg and a hammer and went quietly to him while he lay fast asleep, exhausted. She drove the peg through his temple into the ground, and he died.

22 Just then, Barak came by in pursuit of Sisera, and Jael went out to meet him. "Come," she said, "I will show you the man you're looking for." So he went in with her, and there lay Sisera with the tent peg through his temple—dead.

23 On that day, God subdued Jabin, king of Canaan, before the Israelites. 24 And the hand of the Israelites pressed harder and harder against Jabin king of Canaan until they destroyed him.

STORY #7: Women Courageous and Fearless

WITHOUT WOMEN IN OUR lives, the world just wouldn't be the same. Jesus was brought into the world by a strong woman, and even at the beginning of humanity, God put and chose a woman on Earth to accompany man. There are many Bible verses about women that show their strength time and time again during hardship, life's most fearful moments, and in happy times, too. God made women in his image for a special reason, and the word of the Lord reminds us of this fact each and every day through specific verses and stories passed down of powerful women like Queen Esther.

In the bible, courage is also referred to as "good cheer," which means boldness and confidence. Throughout the Bible, God commands us to fear not, to be of good cheer, and to have courage in our life. Sometimes we doubt our own strength and conviction but can turn to scripture for the encouragement to live in good cheer and trust in God.

A woman of faith is fearless. She fears no evil, for God is with her. There is no ambiguity, no uncertain triumph in her life. She can live a principle life because of the teachings and doctrines of the perfect teacher, the Master. A woman who is fearless has the courage to do what is right and avoid what is evil. A woman of faith loves the Lord. She wants him to know it by the life she lives, by the word she speaks, and by her every action. A woman of faith is also blessed by faithful men in their life.

Women in the Bible who were bold and faithful in their Spirit-led interventions and, in their womanly way, were mightily used by God. Queen Esther showed godly-feminine courage.

Esther was a brave young woman who saved her people from being wiped out. She was a beautiful Jewish orphan girl who became the queen of Persia around 475 b. c. after winning a beauty contest. She was able to save the Jewish people in the Persian Empire from being destroyed. Her story is in the Bible in the Book of Esther.

Esther's cousin Mordecai saved the king's life once when two men in the palace tried to attack him (Esther 2:21-23). And he also played a big part in helping Esther stand up for her people. Haman is the villain of the story. He came up with a plan to kill every last Jewish person. He even built a tower, which he was going to use to hang Mordecai. But Haman got what he deserved in the end. He was hung from his own tower (Esther 7:9-10). After helping to save his people, Mordecai was promoted to second in rank to only the king (Esther 10:2-3). As a Jewish maiden who had become the wife of the powerful king, Esther reached a crossroads of faith. God put Esther in just the right place at just the right time. She was chosen to be the new queen of Persia, where many Jews lived. A few years later, a man named Haman, a high official in the king's court, decided to kill all the Jews—all because of one Jewish man who wouldn't bow down to him. The man was Mordecai, and Mordecai just happened to be Esther's cousin. Mordecai begged Esther to help. But that meant going to the king, and she could have been killed for doing that without permission. God made sure the king was happy to see Esther when she came.

Esther and Mordecai were able to save their people, but only because God planned everything perfectly. He put them where they needed to be. He gave them courage and wisdom. God can't always be seen, but He is always working for the good of His people. Just like Esther, the story of Christine is a strong manifestation and an example of fearless and courageous faith.

This is her story . . .

"I strongly believe living a good life means being able to help others who are in need and who have less. Poverty must lessen. Lifting and aiding one another economically will reduce scarcity. Little by little, we could make anything possible, most especially when we are together . . . Good evening, ladies and gentlemen! Christine Knudsen, 18, proudly representing the USA!"

Joining beauty and brain pageants became Christine's second work. She considered it a succeeding job, for engaging in socio-civic organizations is her first priority. It is her selfless dream since she was a child. Christine was strongly influenced by her parents, who loved serving the community as part of their goals as husband and wife, and they also wanted to pass that mission towards their daughter.

Christine, a typical teenager, is a fine smart, simple young lady with a very curvaceous body and a beautiful, charming face. She was able to study in a high-status university. At a very young age, she already devoted herself to charities, with a sincere desire, which is to ease poverty in the lives of those who are less fortunate and are somewhat left behind.

One bright sunny day, someone with a mysterious look came nearer to her while she was sitting on a blue wooden bench in the park.

"You are Ms. Knudsen, right? Christine Knudsen?" The woman asked.

"Yes, I am. Is there anything I could do for you?" She answered with a smile.

"Hi! My name is Reign Towson. I saw you one time on stage and discovered lots of potential from you. By the way, I am a pageant director. I handle many aspiring beauty queens. I really would like to invite you to be my talent. Just really have to be direct to the point now. You have to start showing off your beauty and brain to many opportunities and wider horizons. You are extraordinary, beautiful, and witty, Christine. I know you know that very well. Only a few are blessed to have such gifts. Do not waste this opportunity. Most importantly, you will earn money from joining pageants. You get to receive a larger amount if you are declared the winner. I have heard you adore charities, and this is going to be a good start for you. Trust me. In case you have made up your mind. Call me through this number. Again, do not waste this chance, Christine. See you sooner. Oh! Not sooner, but see you soonest." The woman expressed.

Christine was hesitant to do what the woman said, for she was not able to join such finer contests before. She thought of it a thousand times, and there she realized something. She believed in making it a perfect avenue for her to further her utmost advocacy, which is to alleviate poverty.

From then on, she started joining big pageants. Christine was able to reach different places and was given a chance to meet new good friends. She had to compete with great beauty and great minds. There were times she won titles, but there were also moments that she ended up being a runner-up, but whatever she received, she was always thankful because her sole purpose was always delivered. Every time she ramped on the stage, her advocacy embraced her entire being. Christine never missed to share it wherever she may be competing. People from different places, listening and watching, were inspired, for they saw how dedicated Christine was in her quest for the difference.

"I could not thank you enough, Miss Reign. The trust and confidence you gave me are indescribable. Thank you so much from the bottom of my heart. Now, I get to help more people." Christine heartily expressed.

After a couple of months, she was pronounced as the ambassadress of Good-Will because of the many awards she gained. Christine was even happier and so excited about what's ahead of her. As the Ambassadress of Good-Will, she was given countless opportunities to help more people, even to the point of reaching the remote and unknown areas. She was able to happily distribute goods, clean water, and medicine.

"Good morning, Auntie. How are you today? I hope you still feel good and blessed despite the situation you are in right now. Have faith in God, Auntie. He will make true of His promises to all. Now, take these humble gifts I have for you." She said.

"Thank you for the assistance, Ms. Christine. Thank you very much. You are so beautiful inside and out. I am glad that there are still people, like you, who still appreciate our existence here. I hope you will never get tired of helping us and others who are in need. You are such a blessing that God sent to this community. May you receive more in life in return for your goodness and service. I will always pray for your journey." An old woman said while having tears in her eyes and, at the same time, tapping the back of Christine.

"Do not worry, Auntie. I will never ever get tired of helping. Seeing people happy with the simple things we give makes me happy, as well. It is very fulfilling inside. This is what I truly love doing since I was a child. Keep safe always, Auntie. You will also be part of my prayers." Christine replied.

From her numerous visits to the people in the said place, she realized that other than food and medicine, people need protection. People from the far-flung areas are very much afraid of rebels asking for payment in exchange for protection, but rebels knew the people there could not give them cash, so they forced them to give crops, fish, and etc. Which made their situation to worsen. Instead of striving hard to feed their families, they now feed the enemy due to the fear of losing their loved one's life, since they were all warned that when they could not give them what they wanted, they get to choose any member of the family and take his or her life. Upon hearing the very sad news and scenario, Christine willingly decided to enter the military, even if that was not part of her dreams in life and knowing that she is not that fast in moving.

She finally enrolled herself in a military task force and faced all the challenges given to her. Her experience inside the campsite was so tough that she almost gave up, but she kept on praying to God for more strength and deliverance, and she brought with her the sole reason why she indulged herself in such a situation.

On her first mission, Christine was sent to Afghanistan. Together with her comrades, they guarded the people against rebels. One night, the rebels attacked. The rebels and the military exchanged gun fires, and both groups suffered losses. Medics arrived to take care of military personnel who are wounded, but someone has to cover them. Meaning, someone has to be left behind to fire at the enemies while the others escape. Christine volunteered to get left behind. It was made clear to her that there is very little chance that she will survive. But she said she was ready. She prayed to God not to save her life, but to save her comrade's life. When the time came, her comrades ran for their lives toward the truck where the medics were situated. Christine bravely and fearlessly fired at the rebels. When she saw that her comrades were already at a safe distance, she held a grenade in her hand and ran towards the enemy, she said a final prayer on her head, and she died with the enemies knowing that she saved her friends' lives.

The story of Christine is like the story of Queen Esther. Their bravery is unmatched. Queen Esther showed great courage by telling the Persian king about a plan to assassinate him, and later, a plan to have all the Jews in Persia killed. With the power of prayer and bravery, she saved her people.

We see God's interaction with man's will, his hatred of racial prejudice, his power to give wisdom and help in times of danger. But there are two overriding themes: God's Sovereignty and God's Deliverance. The hand of God is at work in the lives of his people. He used the circumstances in Esther's life, as he uses the decisions and actions of all humans to providentially work out His divine plans and purposes. We can trust in the Lord's sovereign care over every aspect of our lives. For God's deliverance, He raised up Esther as he raised up Moses, Joshua, Joseph, and many others to deliver his people from destruction. Through Jesus Christ, we are delivered from death and hell. God is able to save his children. Queen Esther teaches the following about courage. Courage stays true to its own. Even in the luxury of the palace, Esther never forgot where she came from. Though separated from her people, she remained a loyal Jew. She never lost her faith or her identity as one of God's people. Courage leans hard on God's strength.

Before Esther went in to ask the king, she instructed Mordecai to gather all the Jews of Shushan. She wanted them to fast and pray for God's intervention. And she and her maids did the same.

When she approached King Xerxes, she went in the strength of her God. Courage acts prudently. Using her God-given wisdom and experience, Esther carefully planned the best strategy for asking the king. She did not blindly rush into the throne room. Instead, she prepared a rich banquet, trusting that God would hear her prayers and grant her an audience with the king. Courage knows which voices to ignore and which one to obey. If Esther had listened to the inner voices of doubt and fear, she would never have dared to go before King Xerxes. Yet she had learned long before to ignore those voices. She knew there was only one still, small voice that mattered. And that was the voice of God. When her very life was on the line, Esther chose to trust God's wisdom and yield her life to him.

Christine, on the other hand, spent her whole life serving others. There was never a time she thought of herself first and regretted all of her actions. Her time, effort, money, and love were given and offered to the less fortunate people. In fact, when she knew rebels were the biggest threat to the people that she cared for, she entered the military. Despite all the hurdles she hurdled, she was able to conquer everything. And even during her service, she chose to be brave and fearless when she sacrificed her own life for the sake of her comrade's safety. She knew in her mind and believed in her heart that God is with her, no matter what happens. Just like Esther, she chose to trust God's wisdom and grace. Her life is worth emulating, and people were more inspired by her story.

Esther and Christine are wise and faithful women who intervened for the good of others, some at the risk of their very lives. They both knew the greatness of their God and had a boldness of speech to match.

STORY 8

OUTSTANDING FAITH

INTRODUCTION

1 Peter 3:3-4 New Living Translation (NLT) Wives
3 Don't be concerned about the outward beauty of fancy hairstyles, expensive jewelry, or beautiful clothes. 4 You should clothe yourselves instead with the beauty that comes from within, the unfading beauty of a gentle and quiet spirit, which is so precious to God.

1 Peter 4 New Living Translation (NLT) Living for God
10 God has given each of you a gift from his great variety of spiritual gifts. Use them well to serve one another. 11 Do you have the gift of speaking? Then speak as though God himself were speaking through you. Do you have the gift of helping others? Do it with all the strength and energy that God supplies. Then everything you do will bring glory to God through Jesus Christ. All glory and power to him forever and ever! Amen

STORY#8: OUTSTANDING FAITH

God's love for all His creation is limitless. God is forgiving and impartial to believers, regardless of their background and past deeds. There is no sin too small or too big for God not to forgive. No single sin is greater than His mercy. There are many women in the Bible whom God accepted and forgave fully with all of his love and mercy. One of the many women who ended following God and showed outstanding faith worth emulating, despite the dark past she had been to, is Rahab.

In the book of Joshua, the life of a faithful woman known as Rahab is presented. Rahab is one of the only two women named in Hebrews 11, the faith chapter of the Bible. Her amazing story portrays how God accepts a person no matter what his or her background is. The life story of Rahab can be found in Joshua 2-6. After 40 years of wandering in the wilderness, it is now time for the nation of Israel to enter the Promised Land. However, they are immediately faced with a great obstacle, the city of Jericho.

Rahab's story exemplifies that God's purpose is not limited to your past. Joshua, now the leader of Israel, sent two spies to scout the city. In the course of the event, these spies happened to come to the place of Rahab, and the King of Jericho ordered these men to be captured. Rahab kept them safe and helped the spies to escape. Rahab is a harlot or prostitute living in Jericho, a Canaanite city. Because of her faith, she and her family were spared from the total destruction of Jericho. Ultimately, she was used by God to play a role in forming the lineage of our Lord and Savior, Jesus Christ. Hebrews 11 has this to say about Rahab's faith: "By faith the harlot Rahab did not perish with those who did not believe, when she had received the spies with peace" (verse 31).

Rahab's life really tells that every opportunity to fear is also an opportunity to trust God. There is no doubt that Rahab could have initially felt worldly fear—the kind of fear that can make a person irrational and unstable in their thinking. However, as the years passed by, Rahab continually has thought of how the God of Israel delivered His people from the mighty Egyptian empire and the two kings of Amorites. The worldly fear of Rahab turned into a godly fear. This type of fear helps a person to think in the right perspective. Fearing God does not mean to constantly cower in terror in His presence. Because fearful forces you have to obey God, it will not produce the right kind of relationship with Him. Godly fear means recognizing the immense power of God and recognizing ourselves as insignificant in comparison to Him. In spite of this, God still chose to send His Son, His beloved and only begotten Son, to die for our sins. Because of this, God deserves our highest respect and reverence. Rahab recognizes that this God has set in motion spiritual laws that when we choose to break, they will break us instead. Because of Rahab fearing God, she was able to begin developing godly wisdom (Proverbs 1:7; 15:33). Rahab feared God, and as a result, her life and the life of her family was spared from the destruction of Jericho (Proverbs 10:27; 14:27).

Rahab's story clearly shows that none of us are insignificant to God. Each one of us is loved by Him, and he sees us all as clean and sinless. He reads every beating heart that we have, and He is more than happy to find a single spark of faith, just like the faith that lit up the heart of Rahab. The faith of Rahab moved her to action. As the Bible says, she was "declared righteous by works." In Roman's 10:17, it is said that faith follows the thing heard. When Rahab heard some valid reports about how powerful and justifiable God is, she put her faith and trust in Him. She became a sincere worshipper and follower of God.

Just like Rahab, Mae has become a good follower of Christ, where she also manifested an outstanding faith despite her past situations in life.

This is her story . . .

"What time is it now? Is this the most appropriate time you should be coming home? Do you still even care about your child and me? Olivia! Answer me! Don't just neglect me! I am talking to you!" The husband asked.

"Wow! The best man on earth is reprimanding me! You deserve an applause! I don't even care. I am doing this for a living. Now, who are you to talk to me like that? You have not also done anything good for this family. At least me, I can look for money and bring food to the table. Also, I am happy with what I am doing. What about you?!" Olivia answered.

This is the usual argument that Mae always hears every single day. She witnesses a chaotic life like this, and she gets used to it. She even gets envious of her friends having a happy and loving family. In her mind, she has questions as to why she experiences such a scenario and as to why her parents are like not.

Mae's mom works in a Night Bar as an entertainer, or prostitute, to be exact, while his dad just stays home to look after her. There was never a day; her parents did not argue about their relationship. Olivia rarely goes home and checks the whereabouts of her daughter. She's very busy with her work and, of course, hanging out with her customers.

Days passed by, Mae's dad decided to leave the house and be with another woman. Before leaving, her dad talked with her.

"Mae, I am very sorry, but I have to do this. I am no longer happy with your mom. I know, she also has another man, besides me. You take care of yourself and your mom. I love you, sweetheart." Her dad expressed.

"Dad . . . Please . . . Do not leave me. Dad, please . . ." Mae cried hard, knelt down, and begged for his father not to leave, but his father kept on walking and leaving until she could no longer see him. Because of what happened, she now considered herself living in a broken family.

One sunny morning, Olivia arrived. She was surprised when she has not met any shout from her husband now. She then looked for Mae and asked father?

"Where's your father? Good thing, he has finally realized that I hate being nagged." She asked.

"Why are you looking for him? You do not care about him, right? He has left us. He is with another woman now. He said he is no longer happy with you. Our family is now broken. Well, I guess we've been broken since then." Mae courageously answered while crying.

Out of the blue, Olivia slapped Mae on her face and said,

"Do not speak to me like that!" she responded. Olivia, in anger, left Mae and went back to the club where she works.

Mae cried hard in anger. She knows she no longer has anyone to lean on now. Her father is gone, and now her mother. This is exactly the reason why Mae took a different path in her life. She embraced the life lived by her mom for years. A friend of hers, Melissa, introduced her to the night-club manager, a club located far from where her mom works.

"Are you sure of this, Mae? You hated this job." Melissa asked.

"Of course, I do, that's was. Before, I knew my mom was an entertainer. I felt like she's very dirty since she keeps on going out with several men. But, I am a different Mae now. If this is the fastest way I could make money to sustain my needs, then I am good with it. I'll give it a try. Good luck to me!" Mae positively responded.

There and then, she started working as a prostitute. At first, she was hesitant because she's not used to it, but as time passed by, she started enjoying it, and especially that she started earning money. She is now used to going out with different men. Mae has now embraced the kind of life her mom lived.

Despite having everything now, Mae's life started to become messy, and no matter how she let herself get obsessed with men's and money, she still could not find contentment.

One day, while going home, her friend in elementary, Clarissa, who is now a song leader in their church, approached her.

"Hi, Mae! It's me, Clarissa, remember?" she asked.

"Clarissa? Hmmm . . . Oh my gosh . . . Clarissa, is that you? You have become a fine lady. How are you? I missed you." Mae answered.

Mae did not know that Clarissa has been observing her for such a long time already. Clarissa did not expect Mae would ruin her life like that. From then on, they started talking and keeping in touch with each other. Time passed by, Mae unconsciously noticed that she's starting to change. Mae shared with her the goodness of God and how forgiving He is to everyone. She introduced Mae to her other friends in the church and allowed her to see God in them through their actions.

Mae then decided to quit her job in the bar and opted to renew her life with God. She realized that her actions in the past were nothing compared to God's mercy and compassion. She apologized to God for all the trespasses she committed before.

"Oh, God. Forgive me for I have sinned against you. Forgive me, Oh Lord. I allowed my body and my soul to be soaked in sin. Please give me another chance; please give me another chance to live again, this beautiful life you have given to me, I have brought shame on it and you, Lord. I will change my life, from now on, with you as my Father, my guide, and my inspiration." Mae prayed in the church while crying.

Clarissa saw her and came near to her. She tapped Mae's back and hugged her. "You are surely forgiven, Mae. I know, you are now forgiven. God is always good. God is merciful and loving. He looks at everyone as very pure and without sin. He is happy now that you are again, with Him, as His child."

"You are God's instrument, Clarissa. I thank God for bringing you to me. Before, when I was working as a prostitute, I asked myself many times how can I ever get out of that situation. And now, I am free. I am finally free from my worst nightmare. Thank you so much for being a friend and a sister. I will forever thank you for everything." Mae responded.

Mae finally felt contentment and happiness, and so she said to herself it's high time to reach out to share the good faith and touch her mom's life. She also wants her mom to change. She looked for her mom and found her in the Night Club, where she works.

"What are you doing here, Mae? I have heard many things about you. You lived my life. I did not expect you to do the same. Well, I guess other people's words are somewhat true that children are a reflection of their parents. Again, why are you here? Do you need money?" Olivia asked her daughter.

"No, I do not need money. I need you. I need you, Mom. Please come home. I will help you change, just like what I am now. I have changed, Mom, because God loves me, and I know God loves you, too. Come back to Him. Please come back to him." Mae convincingly said.

Because Olivia is a non-believer, Mae encountered a lot of difficulties during the entire process of helping her mom renew her life, but she did try hard, every single day and showed an outstanding faith that no matter how difficult it could be, God is with her. Later on, her mom changed her life, as well, and served the church with her. Mae worships and thanks the Lord because she gave her and her mother a chance to be with Him in spirit and in truth again, from being prostitutes to believers of God.

Transformation does happen to every person through action that reveals and develops faith, and not passive belief. This is what happened to Rahab and Mae. A perfect example in the bible is that of the life story of Rahab, who acted on behalf of God's people and is transformed from pagan prostitute to matriarch of the faith. As a woman who exchanges her body for money, Rahab is not a picture of propriety. She even lied in order to protect the Israelite spies, her family, and herself. However, she acted courageously in the face of danger and demonstrated devotion to God. In the book of Joshua, she is transformed from disrespected in a pagan land to revered in

God's community. Regardless of her past, Rahab is redeemed for the present and future. God blessed and transformed her despite her imperfections and mistakes.

Mae, on the other hand, also regained herself from being a prostitute to a believer of God. She also showed an outstanding faith, despite all the things that happened to her life. Right from the very beginning, Mae lived a chaotic life. She's used to having parents who always quarrel over things. Her mom's job, which is being a prostitute, made her life more miserable, which she also embraced when her dad left them. She chose the path lived by her mom. Just like Rahab, she exchanges her body for money, just to provide all her needs, and also to somewhat forget being alone in life. Despite everything, she still could not find contentment and happiness. She knew something was lacking in her life. She was knowing that God moves in mysterious ways. God used Clarissa as an instrument to change Mae. Right there and then, Mae was introduced to the goodness of God. She apologized for being a great sinner and for ruining her body and soul. She changed her life and was more than thankful to know that God has forgiven Her. Moreover, she realized her mother also needed God's healing of the soul, and so she tried her very best to also lead her Mom to come home to God again. Mae manifested an outstanding faith in her everyday battle against her past. God has saved her and her mom from their dark past. True enough, God looks at them as clean and pure.

I strongly believe God is much more interested in how we act and treat people than what we accomplish in life. He is most interested in every person's heart, and a lying heart is not a pleasing heart. Our God is a merciful and loving God. He looks at us as clean and underrated without a spot or wrinkle on our soul.

STORY 9

STRONG PORTRAIT OF BIBLICAL WOMANHOOD

INTRODUCTION

Please help me share her as you read each line in the stories. The way she makes you feel in each title topic of stories conversation. She makes you feel belonging, that represents our purpose, our strength, and our reason for living.

But despite her fame in life, there are many things about her that most people don't realize. There are also some assumptions about her that have been distorted, either by the men's propaganda against her, which was perpetuated or simply the lies of history. But I do feel there's no proper way to comply with or believe all assumptions are not important. However, one wonders why these ideas got to them and why they listen.

But God knows all and sees and hears the entirety in advance, which aids me to be witnesses to the actual stories written about women in this book. Keep in mind the storylines must be read in context and not alone, to get the meaning and not be obscured. But I have no wish to lead you astray from the truth about her and pray I didn't. In many ways, I am a simple man—the Lord said it in His Word.

STORY# 9: Strong Portrait of Biblical Womanhood

GOD CALLS EVERY WOMAN to remain strong and to live his teachings. In the bible, men become the most-talked-about. However, there are a handful of women or females who lived a Godly life in the Old and New Testament. Women are described to be individuals with lots of capabilities. They did not just wait for good things to happen. They worked hard to attain such. They were very faithful to God.

One perfect example for a woman who has shown a strong portrait of biblical womanhood is Priscilla. She is also called Prisca. Priscilla was known to be a Jewish individual who was then transformed and embraced Christianity. She was used to being mentioned in the bible, together with her husband. Priscilla and her husband became loyal and faithful to God. They were great servants. They work together for the glory of God and to be able to influence others and develop a strong faith. Her husband, known as Aquila, also became a good example of great lovers. They were very devoted to their marriage and to each other. What they both promised in the altar of God was really lived upon, day by day. They both observed equal partnership. None of them is above or superior, except having and considering God as their master. They were very useful preachers and influencers of God's gospel. In the New Testament, Priscilla spent time with the Apostle Paul. She and her husband Aquila didn't only endangered their own lives for the sake of Paul but also showed an example of a Godly marriage.

We first meet Priscilla in Acts 18. She sometimes also goes by the name of Prisca (2 Timothy 4:19). She and her husband left Italy by the decree of their emperor, who ordered all the Jewish people to get out of Rome. The Emperor did so because of a certain man named Chrestus who had caused havoc, according to Suetonius. In 41 AD, Jews couldn't meet in Synagogues and were eventually expulsed from Rome in general on account of Chrestus. We don't exactly know what Chrestus did, but this article argues the disputes arose about Jesus.

No matter what the case, Priscilla and Aquila meet Paul in Corinth. The three of them bond over the trade they all do as the main job (Priscilla and Aquila) and a side hustle (Paul): tent making. So they make tents together. Or, as this article argues, the more likely worked with leather. Later, they set sail together toward a place called Antioch (Acts 18:18) and continue with him to Ephesus, where they meet an apostle named Apollos. Apollos has a great talent for public speaking but doesn't quite have his theology correct, so Priscilla and Aquila guide him on some of the teachings.

In Ephesus, the two of them establish a church in their home (1 Corinthians 16:19). During the Early Church, many Christians would hold church in their homes. Throughout their ministry, the couple exemplifies kindness, hospitality, and hard work, no matter where God plants them.

Just like Priscilla, Ana also manifested a strong portrait of biblical womanhood.

This is her story . . .

"I, Ana Hilton, take you, Dexter Johnson, to become my lifetime partner. I will always love and take care of you, no matter how zig and zag life could be. I will be with you always, through thick and thin. Rest assured that only death can separate us from being in love with each other. This is my vow to you." Anna expressed with tears.

"I, Ralph Johnson, take you, Anna Hilton, to become my lifetime partner. I will always love and be with you, be it better days or bad days. I will be the same Anna you knew, right from the start. Only death could keep us apart. This is my vow to you." Dexter responded with tears.

It is an emotional yet joyful celebration for the newlywed. After all the struggles they have been through; finally, they are now together as one, and only death could separate their love from each other. It is very evident to the faces of the couple how happy they are on this special occasion in their lives.

"This is the most memorable day of my life, my love. After so many years, I am very thankful to God that He gave us what our hearts really desired. I really prayed to Him. And you also know that. True enough, that when you pray hard and learn to wait for God's answer, He will truly give it to you. I am so glad to call you now, my husband, Ralph. I love you so much, my love. Thank you, Lord, for this blessing." Ana happily said.

"If you are happy now, know that I am happier. You are now my wife. We are now together. I would thank the Lord for the rest of my life. I also prayed hard to Him that the right time would come, which He would grant me, you, and know that prayer became a reality. You are now my wife, Anna. Know that my love for you will have no expiration. I will take good care of you, no matter what happens, and we will continue the practices we were used to doing and showing the people when we were still in a boyfriend and girlfriend relationship. I love you so much, too, my love." Ralph replied with glee.

Years back, Anna and Dexter had to face a tough situation just to be able to have the relationship that they have right now. Anna came from a wealthy family, while Dexter was only raised from a poor family. They both serve in a charity house as volunteers. They both love taking care of people and spreading care and love. Since Anna was born rich, she was used to sharing her blessings to everyone. She grew up to be kind and hospitable. She has a good heart. Dexter, on the other hand, was accustomed to a simple yet loving family. He was taught by his parents to help others without doubts, give without questions, and love without expecting something in return. These two were both believers of God. At a young age, they already practiced their faith and spread it to others.

Because of the life status which they differ, Anna's family did not like Dexter. They wanted another man for their daughter. They did not like Ana, whom they have sent to a renowned University and whom they raised well, will only be married to a poor guy. However, Ana really loved Dexter. Dexter also loved Ana that much. They both knew everything's going to be hard for their relationship, but they fought for it. Because of their desire to really be with each other and to get married, Anna somewhat experienced a rich to rag life. In spite of this, she was very willing to embrace anything just to be with the man he loves the most. Her parents did not give her any support at all; right from the start, she chose Dexter over them.

Now that they are already married, Dexter built a small house for them. He was very hands-on in terms of their shelter and anything for her wife. He works hard every day just to support their needs. Even if they are living a simple life, very far from what Ana was used to having before, they are very happy and content. They know that when they have each other, and of course, with God as their source of everything, they can achieve anything that they want.

In the village where they live, all the people know them for their goodness and kindness. They share anything that they have to others when people need assistance. They are also known to be very religious and God-fearing. In their small house, they have a little where they gather kids from their neighbors to join some catechism. They believe that the right time that God's words should be instilled is at an early age. Kids love to go to their house to listen to Ana's sharing of beautiful words about God.

One morning, Anna's attention is caught by a child looking so hungry and tired, walking down the street near their house.

"Alms. Alms. Alms. Please help me. Anyone here who has water? I am very thirsty. Do you have food? I am so hungry. Please help me." The child cried for help.

While his husband is at work, Anna approached the child and brought it to their home. Since the child looked so rugged, she asked him to take a bath. She gave him small clothes of her husband and turned it over to the child. She also prepared good food for him. The child looked so happy and grateful to her goodness.

Ana asked the whereabouts of the child and said he is lost. However, the child knew he came from afar. In the meantime, Ana assured the child that he could stay with them for as long as they have not returned him yet to his parents.

When her husband Dexter came home, she told everything to him. Being very supportive, Ralph supported her wife's decision. While they're still looking for any information that could lead to the child's roots, they took care of the child with love. They offered the child a home, a companionship, and a life with God. Anna did her very best to teach the child the goodness of God, the father, and God's Son, Jesus. In a short span of time, the child learned to be God-fearing and loving. As time passed by, Ana and Dexter also learned how to love the child. He somewhat like became their own child.

Until one day, a woman knocked into their door and looked for the child. The child came out and uttered the word, "Mama." The woman expressed her thanks to the couple for taking good care of her son while he's under their care. She held the hands of Anna and said that she could not thank her enough for the goodness that she did to her child.

Before saying goodbye, the child hugged Anna and Dexter and thanked them for everything they did for him. He whispered these to Ana's ear . . .

"You are just so wonderful, Tita, Anna. Thank you for teaching me everything about God and the good values you instilled in my heart. I will never forget you. Goodbye."

Upon hearing those words, tears fell down from Anna's eyes. She was a bit sad because the child had to leave, but was happy because she knows that she did not miss to do anything she could for the child.

To ease the feeling of hurt, her husband embraced her and said, "We already did our part. I am very proud of you, my wife. You never failed to be good to others. I know that child will be blessed by God, and time will come that we could see him again, soon."

The life story of Priscilla and Anna is a strong portrait of biblical womanhood. They both showed the values of being faithful to God and being kind, hospitable, and loving to other people. They also made their simple homes to become the place of Jesus for others.

Christians can learn a great deal from this woman from the first century AD. God Can Accomplish Great Things During Difficult Circumstances. The origin of Aquila's name shows they likely came from a prominent family in Rome. The fact Claudius ejected them gave them every reason to worry that God had thrown them into a frightening situation as strangers in Corinth. Not to mention they have to move around frequently from Rome to Corinth to Antioch and Ephesus.

Nevertheless, God continues to move through Priscilla. She helps Apollos refine his theology so that he can preach the Gospel more effectively. She originates from a church in a difficult area in the ancient world and helps it to thrive.

God Can Use the Talents of Anyone. Most women didn't work in the ancient world, and yet, Priscilla had a mastery for tent making, hospitality, and theology. God used all three to help bring many to him.

The misfits, the outcasts, and those who don't quite fit a certain mold are often the ones God chooses in Scripture. This applies especially to women in Scripture. He has the women find the tomb, give birth to the Savior of man, lead Israel as a formidable judge (Judges 4), and to accompany apostles on their journeys.

God Values Hospitality and Loyalty. Priscilla may not have had a Jewish background, but she follows her husband into Corinth. From riches to rags and making tents, she continues to remain faithful to her husband, exemplifying the common mantra for marriage "for richer or for poorer."

She also provides for Paul, and those she later has in her house for church, to the best of her ability. We don't know how quickly Priscilla and Aquila had to flee from Rome, but expulsions of this kind often mean they didn't have a chance to grab all of their material possessions. They likely had to start at square one or something close to that. But whatever they have, they share. They offer Paul a home, companionship, and friendship during his journeys.

Ana, on the other hand, similarly lived the life that Priscilla had before. She came from a rich family but opted to become poor when he chose to be with her husband. She learned to live a simple life with him and found happiness and contentment. Ralph and Ana manifested a strong marriage in their life. Their love for each other is incomparable and selfless. In the village where they live, they practiced hospitality and kindness, most especially when a lost child came into their home. Ana took care of the child, loved him, and taught him the values he could use for the rest of his life. Being faithful to God was also taught to the child. Ana and her husband did everything they could for the child to feel loved and cared for while he was with them. True enough, in the end, before the child bid goodbye to them, he thanked Anna for everything she did for him, most especially in introducing God to him.

Ana's life is something to be looked up to. It is something that gives lots of lessons and points as Christians. For a married couple, the relationship that she has with her husband is also very ideal. They both placed God as the center of their relationship.

All Christians, whether men or women, can learn a lot from the life of Anna and Priscilla. They both exercised extreme hospitality and kindness, even when they had lost their riches. Nevertheless, they continued to walk faithfully with God and their husband and excel in whatever task they are into. It is from their story that we can appreciate the importance of loyalty and obedience to our calling.

STORY 10

FEARLESS IN FAITH AND GRACE

INTRODUCTION

King Solomon pointed out that if we know the truth about reality, "Then you will understand what is right and just and fair—every good path. For wisdom will enter your heart, and knowledge will be pleasant to your soul. Discretion will protect you, and understanding will guard you." (Proverbs 2:9-11, NIV).

A strong woman should be celebrated, for all her beauty and achievements, and physical and mental strength should be counted among the strongest. It is something that a woman must work hard for, something that forces her to set a goal and practice the discipline necessary to achieve that. And that is a beautiful thing. It is something to be respected and cherished, not looked down upon or left to just men.

At the end of the day, women are simply awesome. They are diverse, dedicated, confident, and most certainly beautiful. Too seldom do people seem to recognize this, and that's a shame. Let's start seeing beauty in more than one form.

STORY #10: Fearless in Faith and Grace

GOD DOES NOT LOOK into our mistakes, our physical appearance, and our individual mistakes. He sees our entire being as clean and pure. In the bible, many women are mentioned for being brave, faithful, courageous, and selfless. They have become heroic and strong in their very own way. Throughout the Bible, there are many stories of strong and heroic women. Even at present, through their stories, they are trying to touch our hearts to be able to live a Godly life, just like what they did in the past.

A good example of a woman who has become fearless in faith and grace is Abigail. Her life story begins in 1 Samuel 25, during a time when people like David and also his kinsmen were escapees from the very King Saul. Repeatedly, Saul's army hunts for David, but he continually evades them. Although not a well-known character in the Bible, scripture describes Abigail as a beautiful, intelligent woman who was in an arranged marriage to a wealthy, yet callous man named Nabal.

David has been in the desert on the west end of Sea of the Dead near a large area of Nabal's land where he was raising sheep and goats. Knowing Nabal was in the area, David sends some of his men to greet him and request provisions. They approached Nabal with good wishes and peace. They also tell Nabal that they protected his unarmed shepherds in the fields from desert raiders. Abigail's husband, Nabal, who had been known as cruel and unkind, insulted the servants of David, questioning David's identity and his power. Because of what he did, the servants did not give him his request, which is food. His words reached David, which caused the king to be very angry at him, which led him to make a decision, which was to kill him and all his protectors. Four hundred of David's men were asked to head to the camp of Nabal. When this act was known by Abigail, she hurriedly looked for ways to lessen David's anger. It was gathering some supplies of food as a special present to the King and to all his men. Nabal was so clueless about his wife's actions in order to save him. Abigail met David and gave him all the food supplies. She begged for his husband's safety. She said to him that Nabal's character is really like that. Even she, as a wife, gets hurt by his actions. Nabal was described as a fool. Upon hearing all her explanations, David decided to stop the plan. David knew that God's intervention was with Abigail as she faced him.

Time passed by; Nabal died because of a heart attack. When David knew about this, he immediately gave a message to Abigail to be his lovely wife. Right there and then, Abigail agreed. Abigail's wisdom and action saved Nabal's people from disaster. However, being wise in itself may not be sufficient in some situations, and one must act upon their wisdom. At high risk to herself, she requested for his husband's safety to David. She offered herself in great danger, just for her husband to live. This is like the sacrifice of Jesus in the cross to save us from all our sins. Abigail simply means the cradle of joy. Her life with Nabal was like a nightmare. Her love for him was just wasted. Her joy came from God, who became his source of strength and companionship.

Just like Abigail, Evangeline also showed fearless faith and grace in her life. This is her story . . .

"Evangeline? Evangeline? Evangeline?!!! Where are you? Come here! Where is my meal! I need it now. Faster!" Cornelio shouted.

"Cornelio? I am here in the garden. Please wait. I am coming." Evangeline hurriedly replied while going back to the house.

"Who told you to be in the garden? Whenever I call you, you should be here right away. I do not like to wait for a long time." He added.

Cornelio started hitting her with a utensil in her head.

"Stop! Please stop. That's painful. Please. I am begging, Cornelio. Please stop hurting me."

Cornelio did not bother to listen and just continued hurting her. Tears really fell down from Evangeline's eyes while convincing and begging Cornelio to stop hurting her.

"I am sorry, my husband. I will not do it again. Here . . . Here's for our dinner. Vegetables and dried fish." Evangeline worriedly responded.

"Is this what we're having for supper? You know I hate this food. This is trash. I do not like these. How could you let me eat such trash!" He angrily exclaimed.

Cornelio threw the vegetables and dried fish to the trash bin. Evangeline tried to stop him from doing it, but she was just neglected by him. She had nothing to do but cry while watching her cooked meals placed inside the trash bin.

"Now, you are crying. Whose fault is that? Go to the market now and buy something for you to cook for me. I want something delicious. Move now. The next time you fail me, I will never ever come back home again, and you will spend the rest of your life here in the house alone. Do you understand?" Cornelio said to his wife while pointing fingers on her head.

Upon hearing what her husband said and after being yelled at, Evangeline knelt down and cried hard. She quickly stood up, grabbed her basket, and went immediately to the market. While on her way, her tears did not stop falling. She knew that she did not fail to be a good wife every single day; it is just that her husband does not know how to appreciate her efforts and just neglect her.

Evangeline and Cornelio have been married for fifteen years now. Since they lived together, Cornelio has been very cruel to him. When they were still lovers, he was not like that. Cornelio has been very caring and loving to him. This is the very reason why she fell in love with him, but everything changed when they got married. Other people's statements were somehow correct that you get to know more the person better when you live under the same roof. For fifteen years, Evangeline experienced cruelty with her husband. Sometimes, she even gets physically abused when Cornelio dranked. However, despite his cruelty, Evangeline did not leave him. Instead, love him more. Evangeline constantly prays to God to change the attitude of her husband. She prays every minute and every hour to touch her husband's heart and renew his soul. She strongly believes that one day, her husband would still change for the better.

To lessen her sadness at home, Evangeline puts her attention to sharing God's words to the youth in their place. Every afternoon, she spends two to three hours visiting the houses of their neighbors and teaching the youth about the goodness of God. People in their place appreciates everything she does and considers her as a good person. Well, aside from being beautiful and intelligent, she's been very helpful to others, and God-fearing. People even wonder why she still chooses to stay with her cruel husband, knowing that she could have lived a better life without him. For Evangeline, she would not leave the man she promised to spend the rest of her life with, in the eyes of God.

One sunny morning, Evangeline waited on the porch for the coming of her husband. Cornelio did not go home overnight. Evangeline, who was very worried, haven't slept the whole night thinking and waiting for her husband to come home. She was very happy when she saw her husband approaching their house, but at the same time, a bit sad because he's drunk again.

"Where have you been, my husband? Cornelio? Where have you been? Come here. I'll change your clothes. I already prepared clean clothing for you to wear. Your food is also ready. Come here now. You know Cornelio, I have been so worried about you. Thank God you are safe." She said.

Sad to say, Cornelio did not answer her. She seemed to be absent in his eyes. Tears started to fall, but she still took care of him until he fell asleep. She changed his husband's clothes, cleaned him, and made sure he's totally fine. She also placed her husband's meal near him so that whenever he'll be awake, his food is ready, and he need not call her quickly and be angry.

This is the usual scenario that Evangeline is facing in their marriage. In spite of this, she remained faithful in God and strong for her family. Whenever her husband speaks undesirable words against her, she just tuned them into encouraging words that she needs to do better every minute as a wife. Even if it is painful on her part, she still cares and loves her husband so much.

One night, her husband unexpectedly shouted because of intense pain in his stomach. She immediately brought him to the hospital.

"Help! Please help! Evangeline! It is very painful. My stomach is like burning. Please help me, Evangeline!" He exclaimed.

The doctor advised him to stop his vices and to just be at home to be able to get a good rest. Cornelio was also asked to observe a healthy lifestyle. From then on, he just stayed at home. That moment became an eye-opener for him. Every time he calls his wife and asks for something, her wife always gives him what he wants. Evangeline tirelessly takes care of Cornelio, day and night.

One late night, Evangeline started praying, expecting that Cornelio is already in a deep sleep, but she did not know that he was just listening to her. These were her exact words . . .

"Oh Lord, I thank you for keeping my husband safe. Thank you because you did not leave us. Thank you because we are still together under one roof. You know how much I pray that one day, he would be back to being the man I first knew years ago, how I missed that man so much. You know how much I love my husband. Thank you for being with us, always."

Upon listening to her wife's prayers, Cornelio felt touched for the very first time and regretted everything he did to his wife. From that experience, he started to change his life and the way he treated his wife. Evangeline was very glad and thanked the Lord, for she knew God helped her and listened to her prayers.

"My endless thanks will be with you, Oh God. You never left me all throughout my journey of being a wife. I thank you for sustaining me every single day and for giving me enough strength to endure my husband's abusive acts against me. Thank you for still letting me his goodness despite all the things that he did to me. You know how much I love my husband. I could not repay you for your goodness. Again, thank you for this wonderful blessing. I am just very happy about how he starts to change. May you continue to be with us, always. Amen."

Both Abigail and Evangeline manifested a fearless faith and grace. They trusted God with all their hearts as they faced the life they had experienced. Struggles they encountered were not easy, but they stood still, knowing that God is with them, no matter how shaky things had been.

Abigail and her husband seemed to be not a good match. In spite of this, she did not think of it as a loss. Instead, she continued loving and caring for her husband. The scenario she was in allowed her to become more faithful and prayerful to God. Abigail taught us a lot of things in life, which we can really follow. These include having a good attitude, being decisive, being courageous, being wise on things and discerning, as well, being humble, being trustworthy, being truthful, and being faithful. In the bible, it is clearly stated that it had been through a lot. Her life can somewhat be compared with a plant that needs to be always watered. She needed love and care from her husband. What she got in return were abusive acts and the feeling of being unwanted. It was really tough for her. Good thing, she has God.

She never felt alone because she knew right from the start that God is always with her, no matter what happens. Every single day, she keeps on praying for her husband to change. She got to respond to things positively, even if things did not go her way. Even when she was being mistreated by her husband, she still has a forgiving and loving heart. She knew God is in control of what was happening around. Abigail accepted the situation that she's in and embraced it with full hopes and prayers. When her husband happened to die, God placed her in a situation where she really dreamt of having—to be in a happy family and to be treated well as a wife. She became the wife of David. True enough, she was given so much love, which she did not even experience before when she was with her husband. Abigail taught us that in the end, we will still become victors of our own battle. We just really need to make sure that we will consider

God as our strongest weapon. Abigail truly lived a Godly life. She is really worth emulating.

Evangeline, on the other hand, showed a strong manifestation of good discretion beautifully in form. Evangeline and her husband somewhat experienced a mismatch in their marriage because of Cornelio being cruel while Evangeline being loving and caring. For fifteen years, she embraced the cruelty of her husband, from receiving hurtful words from him and from having bruises because of being physically abused, most especially during the times her husband gets drunk. Despite having such a husband, she preferred being joyful in the hands of God and in teaching and sharing God's words to the youth in their place. Every single day, she developed such qualities as discretion, wisdom, courage, and faith as she faced her marriage journey. Even if for other people, Cornelio did not become a fit husband for her, Evangeline still sees him as the right one for her. She chose him and promised the Lord to be with him for the rest of her life. There was never a time Evangeline failed to pray to God that one day, her husband would change. With God's goodness, he listened to her plea. He granted her prayers. Her husband started to change and appreciate her for being a wife when he encountered a health problem. That time he saw how selfless his wife is, just to make sure he's always fine. Evangeline was very thankful because, finally, her husband, Cornelio, became a changed man, in her eyes and in the eyes of God.

The life story of Abigail and Evangeline tries to teach us to become fearless in faith and grace, for God will never forsake nor leave us, no matter how hard the situation could be.

STORY 11

DILIGENT WOMAN

INTRODUCTION

At birth, each of us starts life standing before a blank canvas, not knowing the material on which God uses to create us for the duration of our earthly existence. God creates a picture of our life, which will leave an imprint on those around us. To me, there's no better imagery than a woman. She initially displays the emotional aspects of loving one another besides our differences. It may not be a clear picture now but is going to be—the imagery on canvas will continue to emerge as time goes on.

Who has ever lived or will live will know her statues are put in places for us to connect with the supernatural realm where God lived. As a queen/ King, she is needed to provide for deity so they would protect humanity.

STORY #11: DILIGENT WOMAN

BIBLICAL HOSPITALITY IS ABOUT extending a hand in friendship to another of God's children. Martha manifested biblical hospitality by being a diligent woman.

When we hear about Martha in the Bible, it is often in a negative way. She was the sister of Mary, who was so busy with meal prep and homemaking duties that she wasn't focused on her revered guest, Jesus. But, Martha also displayed great faith in God, as well.

In Hebrew, Martha is translated as mistress or myth. This originates from the verb "marar" which signifies being bitter or being strong. Therefore, the name Martha simply means "Mistress," "Land-Lady," or "Lady Boss." Martha is believed to have lived in Judaea Province, specifically in Bethany. She is found in both Luke and John. In Luke, his life story was written between the years 80 to 90 and in John, between 90 to 100. Martha is the sister of Lazarus and Mary. She's also been connected to Simon the Leper, as she's known as his wife.

Martha is believed to own a home and was the one assigned, among the siblings, to carry the responsibility of all connected with any single household activities in her home. She was really considered as a personal friend of Jesus. Martha was mentioned in the bible in three places. The first one can be found in Luke 10, where she was in her home, and she hosted a special meal for Jesus and all His disciples. Jesus is said to be loving to Martha's family. With that, Martha was very busy preparing for Jesus' meal and for others and also was trying to be the most caring for her guests. On the other hand, her sister, named Mary, just sat down and simply listened to Jesus, which caused Martha to get annoyed.

In Luke 10;40, it says that Martha was so distracted by all the preparations that she made and because she just saw her sister doing less than what she's doing, she then said to Jesus if He does not care about her sister letting her do all the work. More so, she commanded Him to tell Mary to help her. Since Jesus is very understanding, compassionate, and also kind, He understood Martha's point. He knew what's truly in her heart. Jesus knew Martha was just troubled and, most importantly, tired. Right there and then, He told Martha to not worry about everything that she's doing, most especially the preparations, because what is more important is spending time with Him, which is really needed and which Mary was doing all along.

The second time any person could read about Martha is in John 11, where the death of her brother, Lazarus, happened. Before her brother died, she ran for help to Jesus, but He was already late when he arrived. Lazarus was already dead. Martha showed that she really has great faith in Him, which will heal his brother. She was sad when her brother was not saved but was assured by Jesus that her prayers would be answered. She was really rewarded when Jesus resurrected his brother after four days.

Lastly, we get to come across Martha's life in the bible when she's back as a hostess in their home, honoring Jesus and His disciples. This was the time when Martha and her sister anointed the feet of Jesus with expensive perfume.

Martha's life truly gives proof that her faith is really strong. Just like her, Michelle also showed great hospitality and lived a life of being a diligent woman, despite having some problems with her attitude at first. She was then transformed through God's grace. This is her story . . .

"Jane, kindly entertain our friends in the living room. I will take charge of their snacks. I will cook some fries and make sandwiches for everyone." Michelle asked a favor to her younger sister.

"But . . . Jane, they are your friends. You know them better than I do. I will just stay in my room and watch some videos. Please do the entertaining for your friends." Jane hesitatingly responded.

"What? Are you out of your mind? Your task is just very simple. You will just simply talk with my friends and generate some good talk while I am still preparing our food. It is just very simple, Jane. Don't you like that? Well, you are good at that, chit-chatting with people. Your work is far way easier than mine." Michelle insisted.

"All right, but just for a few minutes, please. My gadgets are waiting for me." Jane answered with no other choice in mind.

While Jane was very busy entertaining her sister's friends, which happened to become her friends, as well, because they used to go to their house, Michelle was very busy in the kitchen. Doing kitchen stuff is not new to her because since she was young, she was already accustomed to doing household chores. Her parents already practiced her at a young age, knowing that she's older than her sister. After a few minutes, she served snacks to her friends. She was only able to speak a few words to them since the time left was spent on eating.

Growing up, Michelle learned to become hardworking in everything that she does. Jane, on the other hand, is the total opposite of Michelle. She just keeps on watching television and doing other stuff, which does not involve helping in doing household chores. Most of the time, Michelle works on things alone. Because of this, it is undeniable that there are times Michelle would complain to her parents about her sister. However, her mom would always tell her to be considerate of her younger sister, and she doesn't want them to fight over such unnecessary stuff. Her mom wants them to learn how to love and appreciate one another. Also, understanding must be observed by siblings, like them.

Every day, Michelle would wake up early to help her mom do the household chores. She helps in cooking, watering the plants, and cleaning the house. She is more than motivated to do such tasks because she wants her parents to always compliment her for her actions, and true enough; her parents would always tell her that she's doing great. On the other side of the coin, her sister would wake up late and just do nothing else but do some leisure activities, since all chores are already done, and food is ready.

One gloomy afternoon, her mom is expecting a visitor. Their mom's closest friend is coming over to their house. Since she does this once in a blue moon, her mom could not contain her excitement and wants to be very hospitable to the guest. Being hospitable is not new to Michelle because her parents already taught her this value years back, and so, it's practiced day by day. Because of this, Michelle's mom asked her help for the preparation.

Knowing that Michelle is good at being hands-on with things, she immediately accepted her mother's plea. She helped her prepare the table, the utensils, and the food. She exerted so much effort for it because she did not want to fail her mom, and she did not want that the visitor would feel unwanted. Unfortunately, after a few minutes, she started feeling tired. When she looked at the corner, she saw her sister, just sitting and watching YouTube videos. Because they were already running out of time, the visitor will already arrive in 30 minutes; she angrily said to her these words . . .

"W-O-W! Look at yourself. Look at what you are doing. While mom and I are very busy preparing some stuff here, you are just sitting pretty there. How lucky you are! Are you not feeling guilty? Don't you even care about what we're doing here? Jane!"

Jane, listening to her sister's words, responded to these . . .

"You exactly know that I am not good at doing the things that you do. I did not offer any help because I do not want to cause a mess and be a disturbance."

"You could have even tried!" Michelle added angrily.

The mother heard their argument and directly interrupted.

"Come here, both of you. Michelle, your sister, is not as good at you, but it doesn't mean it is right to yell at her. You could ask her for help in a polite way. And you, Jane, even if you do not know about many days, you could try. You may ask your sister's help to guide you and to assist you in becoming diligent, just like her. I do not want you to have a misunderstanding. Please try to understand and be patient with each other. You are only two here. Please always bear in mind that God would not be happy when you're fighting. I love you both, fairly, and you know that." The mother said.

From then on, for them to be closer and for Michelle to stop comparing her actions from her sister, their mom would always read them a bible passage every night. Right there and then, the siblings learned to be more hospitable, more loving, and more respectful to one another.

"Sorry, Jane. I am very sorry for the things I said against you. I forgot to speak good things only. May you forgive me. I will do my best to become a better sister to you." Michelle expressed.

"I am sorry, too, Michelle. I promise from now on, to help you do the chores and to be hardworking like you. May you forgive me, too." Jane answered.

The siblings hugged each other and knew that their relationship is renewal, just like the old times, when they were still kids. Their parents were very happy and thankful to God for such a blessing.

The night came. Everybody in the house was already asleep, except Michelle. She expressed her sincerest prayers to God while looking at her family.

"Thank you, Lord, for you have given me another chance to be closer to you. I apologize for always comparing myself to my sister. I will remain diligent in serving my family, others, and most especially to you. More so, help me every day to be humble like you. May you continue to bless my family more."

The life story of both Martha and Jane tries to teach us a lot of things. To be humble is very important. Martha wanted recognition for her good deeds and hard work. She said to Jesus, "Lord, don't you care that my sister has left me to do the work by myself? Tell her to help me!" She wanted Jesus to brag on her and praise her for cooking and preparing the meal. She was probably more than a little taken back when He, instead, gently corrected her, telling her that she is focused on the wrong thing. It's always nice to get a pat on the back, but if we are doing something for that recognition instead of as a service to the Lord or to show God's love to other people, we have the wrong motivation.

Comparing is also not good. In the first story of Martha in the Bible, Martha compares herself to her sister. Martha is doing all the work, and her sister is lounging about chit-chatting away. She laments on the unfairness of it all. Instead of comparing yourself and your lot to others, keep others in your prayers. Jesus is the Kind of Friend We Should All Be. When Martha demanded that Jesus make Mary help her, He didn't reprimand her for talking to Him that way. Instead, he gently corrected her, telling her that she was focused on the wrong thing.

Jesus accepted Martha for who she was. He let her rant and listened but responded with love. Jesus is that kind of friend. We can come to Him, screaming and crying and carrying on and be honest with Him. He doesn't mind. In fact, He loves you so much that He just wants to know what's troubling you. Keeping priorities straight is necessary. When Martha goes off on Jesus, He pretty much tells her to chill and that she is focused on the wrong thing (as I've shared above). Her priorities are completely out of whack. It is good to limit distractions from your life.

Simplify and focus on what He says is important, starting with the most important of all: God. Martha also teaches us to give it to God. In two of the above stories about Martha in the Bible, she was experiencing difficulty and brought it straight to God. Finally, she has been very hospitable. Opening our homes and our heart to others is always a good thing. Hospitality isn't about cloth napkins folded into flowers. It's about making your guests feel welcome by extending grace and love. Biblical hospitality is about extending a hand in friendship to another of God's children.

Michelle's story manifested diligence. However, she started comparing herself to her sister. She observed that her sister Jane would not help her. Instead, she just kept on doing some leisure activities. Because of this, she began complaining, which caused a misunderstanding between the two of them. However, with the help of their mom, their relationship is renewed. They placed God as the center of their relationship as sisters. In the end, Michelle knew what her priorities are, without sacrificing the relationship with her family. She knew God forgave her, as her sister had forgiven her already. Now, they both seek to serve God with diligence and strong faith.

To serve other people and to meet their needs are really great things. May all women embody the life of Martha and Jane. Both of them are diligent and faithful to God. Every day, God really wants us to become productive. God does not want us to be lazy. He wants us to work in His glory. However, God wants us to get rest and a fellowship with Him. It is a very effective way of refreshing our spirits. It is very healthy for the soul. Our relationship with God is very important, so our relationship with other people. We need to love God. We need to love people one another. We need to serve God. We need to serve people. These things are not easy, but they surely will be worth it in the very end.

In our daily lives, it is also necessary to set our priorities. Our priorities at home must be straight. Aside from God, we have husbands, kids, and a lot more things. Removing distractions could be very helpful. Simplify and focus on things. We need to start with the most important person, and that is God. Seeking first to His kingdom and His righteousness will surely place everything in the right path. What's good with Martha and Jane is that they brought things directly to God, verbal and in prayer, their difficulty and concerns. This teaches us to give to God, at all times, whatever we are facing. No matter how small or how big it could be.

STORY 12

THE MOTHER OF ALL LIVING

INTRODUCTION

The mother of all Living to me has always and always will be a woman; some called her Mary and Eve, even then, and now the woman is considered an actual historic symbolical symbol of love.

Scripture References—Matthew 27:56, 61; 28:1; Mark 15:40, 47; 16:1-19; Luke 8:2;24:10; John 19:25; 20:1-18.

A woman is mentioned fourteen times in the gospels, and from references to her, we can see clearly what she did and how she did it. A striking feature in eight of the fourteen passages is that Mary is named in connection with other women, but she always heads the list, implying that she occupied the place at the front in service rendered by godly females. In the five times where she has mentioned alone, the connection is with the death and Resurrection of Christ (Mark 16:9; John 20:1, 11, 16, 18). In one instance, her name comes after that of the mother and the aunt of Jesus. She stood close by the cross with these women, but because of their relation to Jesus, it would not have been fitting to put her name before theirs (John 19:25). No woman, however, superseded Mary in her utter devotion to the Master.

She is written all over the bible: I chose this story about Joanna and Mary, the mother of James, and Jesus.

Trust yourself as you read my thoughts in this story, some things you might find interesting, and become a game-changer in the mind of many. We all think about things and come to our own judgment; this case is no different; I'm just trying to give you something else to think about.

The creator shared with us his image of meaningfulness proportionately of her in and around the present age; her duties, pleasures, understanding, knowledge, strength, love, and beauty combine to make her relevant to humanity.

WOMAN was and is the plan of God, but ideally, God planned for her is to control humanity. GOD created the woman to keep a man in good faith with himself and to share life purposes as oneness, but not being controlled.

I do believe everyone has something in life holding them back from doing what is right when it comes to women.

The Bible portraits, some men may not recognize women as God's masterpiece simply because they may be scared. They feel if women are given their right place in society, they might lose control over her. Some may be capable of trying, and others just would not subject themselves for whatever reason. Hence this problem is not new; it goes back through the centuries, starting far with Adam.

She can transform herself into an objective, meaningful, definitions, and ill-conceived notions that can become known as the superwoman. She is superior in the independence and status of life. In cases, she chooses to pursue a career outside traditional historically society only to be shamed and ostracized and still succeed. Don't be mad at her, be mad at the creator, if you dare!

Today's men are Leary of a woman with intelligence and beauty; two powerful visible factors which she has control of, which was created in her is now revealed! Which will therefore enable her to change society's traditional historically mindful occupied thought? Some say she was created last; in my opinion, she was created first with two embryos, male and female he created them. To procreate the world in God's view and not fit into men's stereotypical idea logic labeling mind, where they think her place should not be. Since you didn't create her, you don't get a vote! This idea stems from the time of Adams!

Adam and Eve. Adam named his wife Eve. God never named her "Eve"—Adam named her Eve. Adam's job was to name the animals, so when Adam named Eve 'Eve', essentially, he's calling her an animal. He's saying: you animal—I'm dominant over you! That's what most men think today they own women.

God gave Adam many things, including a garden, a wife, trees, and other stuff that portrayed a woman symbolically.

More importantly, He was also told to work, dress, and to keep the garden (his church). God presented to him the dos and don'ts of that garden.

Man's duty is to protect and provide for his woman and family from all harm, which includes robberies and also less violent difficulties like cohesion from a snake. The biggest issue here is that Adam utterly fails to protect his woman, so in this worst-case scenario may have caught off-guard when the attack came by the snake.

In my opinion, Adam should have stood up and been a man and said GOD; it was my fault my woman listened to the serpent. If Adam was at home instead of wandering in the wilderness daydreaming thinking about nothing like most men's still doing today, this would never happen. Adam, instead of blaming her for allowing the serpent to deceive her, you Adam should have explained in detail about the tree and the forbidden fruit.

The imaginary conversations Adam had in the fall of man while walking in the garden, he was trying to figure out what to say when asked, what happened to the tree? Adam tried to rationalize when GOD said so clearly not to eat of the forbidden fruit; if so, your eyes will be open. Do, so he blamed his wife! Her love will not have you in an imaginary conversation with the trees and the animals in the wilderness and with you yourself because it's your own imagination, playing tricks on you, not her!

I began several years tracing the rise of 'woman and the fall of man, writing and verbally scribing what the high power gives me to tell about her. It's about her personal struggle for life against the many beastly struggles to find peace during cultivation in the field of ignorance about her.

Now God's word is going door to door in all parts of the world in reader living rooms of their heart, mind, and soul. For the world opportunity for man and woman to prove their obedience to their Creator and return His love. And stop the massive thefts, deaths, and revealed evildoers of ignorance. The ignorance of man does not understand the ingenuity of women; the ignorance of man is not standing up through the times of Adam in defense of his woman.

STORY #12: The Mother of all Living

EVE WAS CONSIDERED AS the mother of all living, for she was the very first woman mentioned in the bible. She was also the very first wife to be known and the very first mother to be emulated. Being the first, Eve was also popular for seeing Satan first and was tempted in order to disobey the words and will of God. Because of disobeying God's commands and listening to Satan's words, she was evicted from the garden where she's together with Adam. That garden is the so-called Garden of Eden, where shame of what had happened and what she chose, without her protector. Eve still remained very hopeful that God would forgive her, and she still persevered through her faith. She became a perfect example of a woman, accepting all the consequences of an act made and a child of God accepting personal responsibilities.

In the book of Genesis, specifically, Chapter II, God Created Adam and decided to give him a companion and, at the same time, a helper. This was made possible by taking one of Adam's ribs and used it to make Eve. She was first called by God as Ezer, which means "help" in Hebrew. It was Adam who named her Eve, which simply means "life." Her name bears the meaning of procreation of human beings. Right there and then, she became Adam's helper and companion. Eve completed Adam's existence. She shared equal responsibility with Adam in the procreation of the human race. Eve was made in the image and likeness of God. Her characteristics were the same as God's. Together, as one, Adam and Eve would continue God's purpose, which is to procreate. Friendship, human relationship, and marriage were brought by Eve in the Garden of Eden.

The knowledge of Eve simply came from the knowledge of Adam, and most especially, from God. At the very beginning, her heart and entire being were very pure. They were created naked but were not ashamed of what they looked like. Both of them had no idea about evil. All they see and know is good. Eve was very innocent about evil. She had no idea about the motive of the serpent. All she knew is that she has to obey God, most of the time. Despite being placed and put over all the different types of animals, Eve still chose to be obedient to the animal, which is the serpent, rather than obeying God. God already warned Adam and Eve not to eat the fruit of the tree, for the tree will give them the knowledge of good and evil. Worst is, death will hit them. Eve was tempted to do such an act, as well as Adam.

Eve's strengths include the following: she was purposely made in the image and likeness of God. She was wonderfully assigned to become Adam's helper and companion. After the great fall she underwent, she was able to bear children. The only person who assisted her was Adam alone. Eve was able to do all her duties as a wife and a nurturing mother, even without taking examples from others, knowing that they were the first persons who were created by God.

If Eve's weaknesses would be the subject, she was really tempted by the serpent. That serpent was Satan, himself. She was deceived by doubting the goodness of God. Eve was out of sight of all the good and wonderful things God offered to them. The Garden of Eden was really made for the two of them. However, she lost contentment. She felt sorry for herself because she could not have a sharing in God's knowledge of what is good and what is Evil. Her curiosity brought her to sin. She allowed Satan to take away her trust in God's power.

Even if Eve shared a very close relationship with God, she failed her faith and trust when Satan confronted her with lies. She even failed to consult her husband's side about it. Eve acted on things without thinking of it many times. She was impulsive and independent in her decisions. Just like Adam, when she was confronted about the sin she committed, she directly blamed Stan, which happened to be the serpent. She had blamed someone else instead of blaming her own self and decisions. She did not take personal responsibility for her own actions. Nonetheless, in the end, she realized that she was wrong. She realized that all that God wants us to do is to choose Him freely and to follow Him at all times and obey Him out of love. Just like Eve, Jenny became a great mother, despite committing errors in her actions in the past.

This is her story . . .

"Who is God? I do not know anything about Him. Does he exist? Did he ever exist in this world? Come on! Stop talking about God! I hate it. I do not believe in him!" Jenny exclaimed.

"Do not say ever again, those words Jenny. God exists. God loves each and every one of us. Despite the past situation you had, I know He still cares for you. He still loves you. "Her dearest friend Amy responded.

Jenny became an unbeliever of God when she was left alone by the time both her parents met an accident. Her parents were killed due to a car accident. Jenny is the only child in the family. She was ten years old when her parents died. She questioned every single day, God's existence because of what happened to her in the past. Even if she had lived in her aunt's place, she still could not feel contentment and still sought her parents' presence.

"Mom . . . Dad . . . How I still wish you were here beside me. I now have my own child. I will make sure I will love her just as you loved me. Good thing my husband is very supportive and loving. But there was never a time; I did not long to see you again how I miss you so bad. They always say God is good, but how come He took you away from me. My life is incomplete because I lost you. I love you, Mom. I love you, Dad." Amy uttered these words while crying.

Her husband, Daniel, noticed her. He came nearer and hugged her. He assured her that everything's going to be all right and that the child would grow well, full of love and care. Before marriage, Daniel already knew the hate in the heart of her wife. He knew her wife hated God because of what happened to her in the past.

However, he still convinces her every single day to go back to Him and to believe in Him again. Daniel knew, from the beginning, that it is really not going to be easy. Nonetheless, he also knew one day, his wife's heart will be touched by God's grace again. He's also thankful because her wife's dearest friend, Amy, is with him in regaining Jenny's faith in God.

After nine wonderful months, Jenny finally gave birth. She was very happy to raise her child well. She named her Athena. Days and years passed by, Jenny and Daniel got another two lovely daughters. They are now five in total in the family. They are both very happy because their family is getting bigger and happier. Until one night, another sad situation happened.

"Daniel? Daniel? Come here. Look at Athena. She looks very pale. Touch her. She's very hot. What will we do? She's having an intense fever. Daniel, hurry!" Jenny shouted because of fear and uneasiness.

"Oh, God, please save my daughter. Let's bring her to the hospital." Daniel responded.

Athena was brought to the hospital. Amy also rushed to the hospital upon hearing the news. Daniel and Jenny kept walking to and fro in the hallway while waiting for the Doctor's feedback.

"You take a rest, Jenny. Take a seat. Everything's going to be fine. God is with us." Amy approached Jenny.

"What? God, again? The last time I experienced this was when my parents were taken away by God. Don't he dare take away our daughter from us!" Jenny became angry.

"Please stop that, Jen. I know how much you love our daughter. I love her very much, too. But this time is not the right time to blame God again. Maybe this is the perfect time for you to ask for help from Him. Please come back to Him." Her husband said these words.

The doctor hurriedly came out and said to them that Athena is in a critical condition. She was having combustion in her entire body. She's getting weaker and weaker. Any time they could lose her. The doctor advised the parents to keep themselves strong in faith, for nothing is impossible with God.

Upon hearing those words, Jenny knelt down in tears.

"I can't lose our first child, Daniel. I can't lose her." She cried.

Jenny hurriedly ran into a small chapel inside the hospital. Daniel hurriedly followed her. He saw her wife walking while kneeling, heading to the altar, while she's crying.

"Please save my child. Please, I can't lose her, just like I lost my parents. Please forgive me for every bad word I said against you. It is because I blamed you for the death of my parents. Forgive me, Oh God. Please forgive me for what I did. Please save Athena. She is our joy. My husband and I can't lose her. We love her so much. Please do not take her away from us, not now. Please give us more time to spend with each other. Forgive me, Oh God. Forgive me. Please forgive me." She continued kneeling down and cried in tears.

Her husband hugged her and joined her in prayer while also crying.

"God, my wife is back to you. She's now with you. Forgive her, Oh God, and save our daughter. Please save our Athena. Please hear our prayers."

A few minutes later, Amy reached the chapel and reported that Athena has woken up. They hurriedly went back to the room where she's in.

"This is a miracle. I have never seen this happen in my entire life. I have been serving this hospital for 30 years already but have not witnessed a miracle like this. You are blessed because your child is given another Chance. Look at her now; I could not find any trace of fever or burning anymore. She's totally fine now as if she has not experienced combustion in her body. She's saved by God. He deserves your thanks. Now, I'll leave you and give you time to talk with your daughter. I'll process your discharge paper." The doctor expressed.

Athena was shocked as to why she's in the hospital. She asked her mom and dad what happened, for she does feel good at all. No pain is felt in her body. She's curious why she's lying on a white bed and why she's isolated in a white room.

"Thank God you are safe now, my love. We were worried about you. Your mom couldn't stop crying, for she's afraid to lose you." Daniel said to her daughter.

"This is because of God's grace, Athena. He saved you. Also, He saved me. God deserves our praise forever. I will always thank Him every day for this second chance He gave us. I love you, my love. Thank you, God, for the unconditional love." Jenny responded.

From then on, Jenny's family became great believers and worshippers of God. Jenny devoted her life in the church now, while being more loving and caring as a wife and as a mother of three.

Eve and Jenny are a great manifestation of being a mother of all living and a renewed faith. The story of Eve in the bible shows a great example of a product of what we call divine creation. She then appeared in the beginning as a woman who is complete and perfect. She never experienced being a child, being a mother, or being a maiden. She directly became an adult, together with her husband, Adam. Eve was the very first female who was born in this world. More so, she became the very first woman to be called a wife. Eve was a great helper and companion of Adam. Since God thought that Adam was still very innocent of the world, he decided to form Eve through Adam's ribs. He did not want Adam to be alone. Adam needed to have a companion for procreation of the human race. He needed someone who will completely love and willingly bear his children in the years to come. God had left them a command, which is to multiply and to replenish the Earth with His creation. At first, the world was sad, so like the Garden of Eden, but when Eve came, everything became happier and more complete. Eve was given to Adam, and that became the start of falling in love with each other.

Eve was created as holy and without sin. She was very pure, for she was created by God with perfection. However, she broke the thought of being sinless by being the very first sinner because of

Adam. Eve was the one who introduced sin to her offspring, which made sins to fold in hundreds to thousands. This happened when she got tempted by the lies of the serpent, which is Satan.

The life of Eve teaches us that all women get to share God's image. These refer to the feminine qualities that are part of God's characteristics. The very purpose of procreation of the human race would not be made possible without the presence of women. Just like what we could gain from the life of Adam, her wife, Eve, tries to impart to us that all that God wants is for us to choose Him freely, to follow him at all times, and to obey Him out of love. Everything that we do can be seen and known by God. Nothing could be hidden in Him. If we get to sin against Him, we must take personal responsibility for our own doings and not put the blame on others. This is what Eve failed to do. When she was tempted by Satan and learned that she committed sin against God, she did not immediately take hold of personal responsibility for her actions and choices; she directly blamed Satan, which is wrong. However, she then realized her mistakes as time passed by and asked for forgiveness from God. Because God has always been very forgiving and loving, she forgave Eve and Adam.

Jenny, on the other hand, was once a believer of God but turned out to be an unbeliever when she lost her parents. When she had her own family, she still did not believe that God exists but still manifested a great role in being an effective mother and a wife. But, one night, she experienced another sad fate. Her first-born child, Athena, encountered a critical condition. Jenny questioned God again but realized she was wrong all along. She then asked for forgiveness and was granted it. God also saved her daughter. From then on, Jenny became a worshipper and a believer of God, together with her family. She devoted her life to the church, at the same time, doing loving and caring roles as a mother of three and as a wife.

The story of Eve and Jenny only proves that God truly wants us to be with Him, in spirit, and in truth, and to trust Him in all of His ways.

The last word, "Restore me unto others."

However, there are parts I left out of The Unfinished Masterpiece (Woman) book, until the last word. I consider this as important as what is left in than out. It's God Fine tuning of Her. As the stories unfolded, God's exquisitely fine-tuned is symmetrically inclusively in the creator of woman. The First Source of life the creator offers potential the three great Absolutes, is actually the Father, Son, and in the Holy Spirit, but the Supreme is both actual and potential, a being of personal supremacy and of almighty power created women's, God did it!

Ending the book in the morning, I can therefore reveal the revelation of a woman in my book and God's visions for her, where all things are of God and are God. As I have said before, view the whole book and don't mind, some parts are contradictory when explaining the origin of unfinished workmanship of women. I am quite careful to acknowledge my first book is not on the same level as everything else I've mentioned in this book; I'm getting better as I'm observing and listening more.

In fact, you have read 12 stories in one book Christians based literature should be considered essential, read. Allow the stories even the less popular ones speak into our hearts today in a new way. Ask the Lord to open your eyes and heart as you read about her to reveal His purpose in placing these stories in the book about women.

In fact, it seems as if the strength of God fundamentalism forces or masses fine-tuned her to create a universe with galaxies, stars, planets and life. The omnipotent and loving God designed and fine tuned woman to improve the way she works and makes her exactly right. I do surely hope I've placed every story, even the so-called boring ones, in the book for a reason.

The creator of her; I wrote about in my book it's not for argument for analogy sake but a poor judgement on your behalf, but the reasoning behind I'm hoping my words about her is not a misuse for probability theory.

But people may try to characterize the argument in a way that is fallacious, but you shouldn't get confused between an attempt to spell out an idea, and the idea behind it. God as a necessary cause and moral foundation of explanations is being pushed back, and is therefore continually in retreat.

So, the point of this paragraph is not to establish an absolute proof of God's fine tuning but to appreciate a miracle of improbable harmony, and ask that question, how could it be?

Growing up, you may consider some books to be rather boring and some parts may become intriguing as you learn the most popular stories, And then of course you fast forward to the next story where you learned.

However, when I began deepening my faith by seeking out the depths of Scripture, about women I realized that Jesus was born in a manger in Bethlehem to a virgin named Mary, only to die on the cross for us and save us all from eternal destruction. Jesus, mothers Mary and Mary Magdalene were identified as being there on that day.

I do think the more you read and study my wordsmith the more the words will begin to sink into the core of who she is. She is one of the many recipes that are treasured by God and handed-downs for man to cherish.?

In a world where some men have forgotten women's exist on earth because of one woman. Some men have made it a primary mission to keep the women at bay and passed down their ignorance about them. But they will fail and understand it's just logically fallacious or argumentatively ignorance on their behalf.

She is understood to be femininely in name and in nature, and great stories are told about her. God's truth, beauty, and goodness are correlated in the Spirit of the Supreme. God the Supreme offers truth, beauty, and goodness for the concepts of divinity.

The creator revealed the divine love of the Father for his children. And having discovered and received this divine affection, women aspire to reveal love to their brethren in the flesh. Such affection is a true reflection of the love of the Supreme.

The beauty of her being unfinished is a moving reflection of sublime radiance, looking like the sparkling tremor of stars and sun on water: a clear expression of God -brightness for us. I want to create words about her that will have you walking and talking to yourself in a way a painter creates the most impressive sight of a priceless piece of art, reaching out beyond reality, in the vision of visibility of God's unfinished masterpiece.

I want to praise you in a way that a poet surpasses the meaning of words for her or his subject and reaches to the mind of the reader with something inconceivable and indescribable in nature. I wish I could describe you even though you're indescribable, just a wonderful phenomenon of a miracle—because that's what you are, something that one can see clearly with the eyes of the heart.

If nobody has praised you for everything you've done, I will honor you right here. If nobody ever applauded you, I will do it right now. If nobody told you that you are an angel with a golden soul, I'm the one who can say it to you a thousand times until you believe it. Although angels don't need praise, applause, or recognition for what they are, they still need to see the effects of their presence on earth. And maybe she needs to feel appreciated to keep their light intensely bright in your life.

Think about it . . .

The Last Word:

You might ask the question, why are all your writing about women or girls. That's a good question? Look around and think about the question you have asked, and the first thought should have come into your mind is woman; if not, it's your choice the deceiver of her.

Yes, I think very highly of women, in my opinion, without women, what else do we have. Women can bring another woman or a man into this world, something to think about. Godlike right?

God's Unfinished Masterpiece: Woman

When I look around there's know other better subject matter to write about other than God, Jesus, Mary and her. All the leading subject matter in my books come to me in my subconscious the time God speaks to me the most because it's my listening hours.

And when I awaken, I add materials for my books, I look around for comparison and contrast to her on earth to write which can be expounded on. Because she is Godlikeness in the form of a woman that brings not one thing to Earth, but all things encompass the planet she's favor by God

I wrote these books to her about her, to share God's love for humanity through her. God wanted us to have the same relationship with all humanity, so she was given.

God spoke in his still voice and said: didn't I give the birds the voice to sing, didn't I give birds there's wings, didn't I give voice to the wind, didn't I give life to the water and in the streams, didn't I give water tears to cry. Didn't I create it all, and I won't let you fall, so be still and live your life in God and Christ".

There are many other books that are currently labeled as masterpieces, but only one written by me that the subject can only be finished by God. Which does not fall out of favor in the future?

I'm sure it is a hard thing to wrap your head around what I'm illustration in this story, and it cannot be dismissed as nonsense, because every time we look at her face, we see in her expression that she is keeping a secret in her mind and the secret is she doesn't want to tell you what actually on her mind because her mind never stopped working.

Maybe she is wondering why she is Unfinished, I do presume to know the reasons why she is unfinished others may have their reasoned, but as you read my book I hope you got to know God's fire is within her soul is only finished when God finished her!

But to tell who taught me to write this book (Jesus) and not fight with my own selfish thoughts to make this book and all of my books important to me, they are more than just finished Wordsworth! All glory to God for working on this (me) and the descriptive words which are valid all come to the actions in life and are validated by Jesus!

I read other novels because I want to read what they say and think about her; I love their storytelling. But what I love the most is how the artistry of creating creates something from nothing. It's my dire hope when you read my book storyline, pages, paragraph, or even just a sentence; your skin tingles with a frisson that leaves you breathless about my insightfulness.

So what is the worth of knowing her plenty? Her fire soul is a spark of fire, a flame that can help you in your walk through life and in all things considered well by God. She can lift and inspire and make you yearn to be great, to be a better person, a better partner, a better father, a better human being. I hope reading my novel about her can spark wonder in your mind and set you on a path to seek out that ineffable flame of inspiration.

Inspiration in her, which allowed us to be chain linked to humankind. When she walked out of Africa to conquer the World, to create amazing works of arts of love in physics and mathematics formulas within a heartbeat of building humanity, remembering she is grounded with the present roots of the almighty God. God knew we needed guidance, which is the key to our greatness comprehension; when a vision is well assembled can be the pinnacle of his greatness. So what's the worth in knowing her? In my opinion .... Everything!

She is unfinished in order to leave more questions than answers." And I believe that is especially true with all women. I'm planning on diving into what I think SHE means here, because this answer may become extremely long, I do recommend looking it up on your own time.

What I think you would learn is you haven't seen this painting in person until now, but when you do, you'll surely cry out. Lord was able to give me a print of her, so I'm happy I have my own piece.

For people looking for something different to fill their evenings, make a start by reading my book or any books. This is an invitation from the author to scan and journey the cosmos scan and peer out at our celestial picture of life in the way she is flayed in the book. A woman is always a sight to see as she is fully illuminated for us to study and love in detail.

She is a reminder that love is in the air, and people of the past used to live their lives much more closely with what was happening. I'm afraid to disappoint her in my scribbler, but she will always rise in the East and set in the West of everyone's life. Following God's direction in searching for a new place to blossom.

Readout loud: May God received the blessing from a reader, seeker, and doers of his Wordsworth in her.

The Beginning Never The Ending!

I had not only the presumptions in publishing my subject, as the sources of my book about women, but hitherto defined all I have explored. I had inwardly and outwardly made the determination to finish this book or to not fail in the attempt.

From my youth, I had been inured to hardships and endurance in life, but when I gazed upon the creation of women in life, she has become so available and loveable. I have wild hope and mingled with humility, in my thoughts as I write, even as the significant worm bores through the hardest oak, I might someday persevere and reach the heart of many in my wordsmith about her.

As I egress profoundly, so fully she is the greatest mystery of roads every traveler travels. I am rarely fond of anything but her.

As time passes, it is like nothing changes in her but the surrounding areas about her. She is the same person I knew when the sun kisses the moon and stars were born. And when all the waterways meet at the oceanfront. I cannot believe anyone in this world has the power to resist the determined will of a woman, so long as health and life remain, the world lives in her. But the failure of every man attempted to defeat her in my research did not astonish me because I knew, in the end, they would fail. I, therefore, are determined to proceed alone, trusting in the guidance of my

Divine Providential God and the powerful purposes about her as I write.

It's true what I first mention, every part of my book is my truth.

It's true the firstborn starts the whole family; what's true is my subject to you. It's true the first fruit started the whole crop; it's true the first seed starts a whole Forest. It's true the first word started the whole book. My research explored her over-time pass and today's, whether she could be considered an early stage of forming a different species of women. Russell says: "The answer is yes. But evolution isn't determined by the same factors in all groups of women, and for the first time, we know why because I have looked at the strength in the relationship between all Women's as she has evolved.

Women still arose from their differences of opinion about her and how she should be interpreted. Much of the confusion and controversy that divides one perspective is the carelessness in interpreting the words written in this book about her. I hope by interpreting the work in this book, getting what God has said in His Word is important because mankind generally does not live by bread alone but by his own word. It's not hard to appreciate how important this book will especially aspire to understand the Word of God through women's.

"She's is and objects loaded with symbolic value,"

"They signify royalty, and a ruler's right to sovereignty—take, for example, the legend of the women in the Bible While this symbolism of power and love is well documented in my book. She has rooted in much more than a mir book! Words can't describe her. Just give homage to her!

Russell believes the woman was an is "a gift from God to institutionalized humanity.

Russell is fairly certain" of his first intuition, about her, and you will be too after receiving the results of her analyses written and confirmed by provenance through me the words of God. "it all should start to come full circle." God did it!

I carefully weighed my undertaking writing about her once more. And before me, the untrodden book about womenfolk; words revealed the obstacles she defeated in the world since her creation. At times I believe a tough journey in the life of a woman's. And therefore, the book, without limits, reservation to all that know and love God's Masterpiece how great she is in God's name.

On the day when you think she's too close, that would be the day she may be now too far, and the day when she is far away, that's the day you wanted her to be close. If you don't know what you have, you will know the moment you lose it.

If you are confused now, how will you fare against the psychological impact of ideological warfare against your own ignorance? If your mind is easily swayed toward understanding her. You have no choice other than to conform to the mainstream ideologues about her in my book.

The Book stories is, about 12 women, but it is packed with powerful messages for all. It is another timely message about women for women but for the world we are living in today. We are surrounded with leaders and articles of information that overload our inbox and TV each day, mostly about men walking according to their own way, and not of God.

Women will find a cure to cancer and all diseases that are killing humanity because she's the birth of life and the sustainability of life. Therefore it would be fitting God-give women the ability to heal others because of her personal connection to the one supreme God. She's a positive perspective towards life, and everything in life that is well granted to us in (her) and her best intention is her willingness to help others makes her the best healer.

Message from the author.

From birth to death, we're asking ourselves (how to?) How to live the life you are given, and at death, you are asking how to live longer? Between life and death, there are thousands of million times you asked how too, we are looking for answers our entire life (how to?). But I have learned so much the time I've lived, and I'm willing to share, that is, "you can't stop what's going to happen." You just have to deal with the (how to?). God made life as simple as possible for us because we're simple people; God wants us to come to him and ask how to?

By contrast, she is the centerpiece of life and for life self-fulfillment and empowerment. In most of all aspects, she is actually a hero. As a matter of fact, she is the quintessence of every race because women are spirituality correctly connected to God. A woman knows she is the one she has to please. Therefore she's the only one who knows her spiritual journey. She has lived up to God's standards. And God is the one she ultimately turned to for help.

Don't compare your relationship with others this will cause you to be unhappy. If you compare your relationship to some other couple's, this will cause pain in your relationship. A lot of couple pain comes from comparison of love. Everyone's life is different. You can only see what other people's show you. There's faces are full of smiles, but you don't know their pillows are wet from wiping tears at night. To live a good life, not to compare, not to envy, this is happiness, in Christchurch and each other.

"I know as of now, I'm a habile author, and I do know there will be a high demand for my book. "GOD did it"

In the beginning, I thought writing another book about God's Masterpiece woman was too much for me to take on one more time. But then I wondered what my horoscope would have said; maybe something like, expect to fail if you are trying to get the creepy old man to change his whole life today. At some point, I considered the man for a moment; I was surprised more than anything, that I have come to a conclusion to write about her. Therefore hopefully, you have come to some understanding about women's reading my book. When you read the stories, what was the first thought that popped into your head? Was it "Ouch!" or OMG?

There's so much truthfully Wordsworth about women in my book. What is important, however, is to understand this book in its entirety with that in mind. I wanted to divide the book into stories parable of reasons; in the hope, words will gradually lift women from the shadow's ignorance and exalts her above your own reasonings.

I asked myself countless questions about my subject line, the most important one, will I get bored writing about her. My answer is never! I'm inspired and committed to working on my book, and then keeping that commitment to myself makes me feel really good, whether I get a few paragraphs or a few pages on any given day. Once I'm tapping away on the keyboard, there's never boredom. It's challenging and intriguing, and I learn something new every day that I write about her.

I'm hoping to deliver an inspirational novel filled with spiritual enlightenment so people can clearly see truly bright jewels that shine. Her persona was once buried under rubbish thoughts and ideas of ignorance. But with the new insights from reading my book, it should be gratifying to know she is the fountain source of drinking, which gives life a new meaning; one can't be asked for more.

We are in a remarkable century, the last half of which, especially the last quarter, has been crowded with discoveries, some of them startling in their approximation to the innermost, or occult world in which woman has not to sway but risen. This century has long been pointed out by scholars, by writers, and by Prophets, as the close of the old and the opening of the new. And in my view of the rapid steps which are taking, you can feel the breath of the news cycle on your cheeks as you watch the deepening hues of the words breaking dawn for women.

"God did it!

At the end of the day, women are simply awesome. They are diverse, dedicated, confident, and most certainly beautiful. Too seldom people don't seem to recognize this, and that's a shame. Therefore let's start seeing beauty in more than one form. Life is far more complex than your "yes" or "no" and "bad" and "worse"

Thoughts or ideas about her. Expand your mind and see the world as it is: a spectrum of existences in her.

With all of that being said and read, I want to sum everything up in three words, "God did it!

Powerful Positive Examples

Biblical women who were poets include Miriam (Exodus 15:21), Deborah (Judges 5), Hannah (1Samuel 2:1-10), Elizabeth (Luke 1:42-45), and Mary (Luke 1:46-55). Those considered prophets include Miriam (Exodus 15:20-21), Deborah (Judges 4:4-5), Huldah (2Kings 22:14-20), Noadiah (Nehemiah 6:14), Anna (Luke 2:36-38), and Philip's four unmarried daughters (Acts 21:9).

Females who governed include Deborah (Judges 4:4), the Queen of Sheba (1Kings 10:1-13), and Queen Candace (Acts 8:27). Deborah is unique in that; as one of Israel Judges, she led an army against the Canaanites.

Other good women include the mother of Samson (Judges 13:23), Naomi (Ruth 1), Ruth (Ruth 1:4), Hannah, the mother of Samuel (1Samuel 1:9-18, 24-28), the Widow of Zarephath, who fed Elijah during the famine (1Kings 17:8-24), the Shunammite woman who gave hospitality to Elisha (2Kings 4:8-38) and Esther. In the New Testament, females of godly character include Mary, the mother of Jesus (Luke 1:26-38), Elizabeth (Luke 1:6, 41-45), Mary and Martha (Mark 14:3-9; Luke 10:42), and Mary Magdalene (Mark 16:1; Luke 8:2; etc.). Others are Dorcas (Tabitha-Acts 9:36), Lydia (Acts 16:14), Priscilla (Acts 18:26), Phoebe (Romans 16:1-2), Julia (Romans 16:1), and Eunice and Lois, who were the mother and grandmother of Timothy whom Paul commended (2Timothy 1:5).

New Testament Female Ministers? 1. Now I commend to you our sister Phoebe, who is a servant (Greek: diakonos) of the church in Cenchrea, 2. Charging you to receive her in the Lord . . . and to assist her in whatever she may need from you . . . (Romans 16:1-2, HBFV)

My personal letter to all women

Please loan me your ears?

Dear women of God's Creation, who will and have read this and feel free and believe in understanding what has been written about you. Indeed, as you were reading you know who has tenderly carried us, together with these memories. I hold you so close to my heart so stay anchored in grace and God's comfort.

I'm sure you have been lied to about nearly everything that has to do with your historical journeyman as a woman. I am sorry for their behavior because I cannot empathize or rationalize with their ignorance. I chose God's love so early in life and had the chance to develop a conscience with the capacity to feel remorse, empathy, and love for all. Still, I know it's wrong on an intellectual level not to love what God has given us in his creation woman, but Sometimes I wish I could be her, but I can't.

When I became a man, I felt my mother love sensitively, on a daily basis, and her love transferred into me. I felt so much love and compassion; it was painful, easy for her. But I was never made to feel like I was nothing or nobody because she knew society would try to do that. But there are people in the world who never experienced love because no one showed or told them about the word love, which is all action-driven.

According to the scripture, the household prepares young ladies and trust-in their mother or father to protect them by screening prospective husbands, for God gave to him that responsibility of protection. (Numbers 30:3-5. That responsibility was not given to the mothers, though her input must be considered.) Any interest a daughter has in any young man should be "run by" her father, if not the mother, before she becomes so emotionally involved that she ignores her mother and father's warnings. However, parents should tell their daughter to place your heart behind God, so if he wants her, he has to go through God to get you.

This gives young men the opportunity to find himself and see if he deserves a Proverbs 31 wife?

Obviously, there will be several objectives that will apply to both men and women, especially men. If you have not heard about a Proverbs 31 woman, here's your chance. The desire of every family is to have a daughter who should be to train up as a Proverbs 31 woman. Her goals to create a happy, secure marriage with a Godly man. She would love to have a loving family in a house where everyone feels welcome to come home. She also thinks a woman must take care of her husband and children (family) firstly while taking care of herself always.

She looks for someone she can communicate with, and without judging who she is. A man of patience and understanding. A man who loves the Lord and knows his place as a man. A man who is there to help pick the pieces when sometimes they fall.

To love her and to accept her as is. She wants to be judged for the things she has done, not for mistakes you may have made. She wants your trust in her and let her know what she feels is right. In my opinion, women are always "right"—it is a matter of love. When she feels alone, empty, or estranged, she wants your eyes to tell her; she's the person you love, and you want her for what she is Proverbs 31 woman.

"To know her is to love her".

However, we hear very little about what should be instilled in sons, so they will deserve a Proverbs 31 wife. It seems that we think boys sort of raise themselves, so the primary emphasis is placed on the girls.

The majority of young ladies prepare for marriage, but young self-absorbed young men interested are primarily in making money and playing video games. A Proverbs 31 WOMAN will not have a self-centered young man, so the boy ends up marrying a self-centered young woman who is attracted to the world rather than to the children of God.

I have also noticed in my research families with appropriate age, boys and girls, are concerned about the girls working at getting her looking for good husbands. But the concern seems to be missing for the sons in the family getting a good wife. In other words, there is not the same emphasis upon the boys seeking a mate as there is upon the girls finding a mate. And why is that, and then we wonder why there are no Godly men for the women who have been properly trained for marriage. Something to think about!

Obviously, the young lady will have to find the man both attractive in personality and in looks. She needs to be drawn to the man, and her parents will need to defer to her taste as they try to help her find the right one, and don't just settle, for any old Tom, Dick, Harry, and scrub!

Fathers of sons, these things need to be trained into your sons, don't turn the boys loose, without guidance and let them raise themselves, you will be a grandfather before you know it!

By God's graceful mercy, we can overcome many things; wisdom dictates that the fewer things that must be overcome, the better the marriage should be. The more similarities, the better chance of a marriage working together smoothly.

Make no mistake, my fellow male readers, we all after something. Many of us just don't acknowledge it—because we are afraid to accept what our heart desires. We are embarrassed; we don't know how to appreciate God's gift. No shame there, my friends, you are not alone in your thoughts but remaining in denial is the problem—always is. When are you in denial, you remain alone!

God Works Within Us

Ephesians 3:20-21

Let these words slowly sink into your understanding: "able to do far more abundantly beyond all that we ask or think" (v. 20)—what an amazing description of God's ability to work within us.

Happiness is the only thing on earth that cannot be paid by diamonds, gold, or money. Money and love aren't the same things; see, the more you spend money, the less you have, the more you spend love, the more you get in return.

On my walk today, I saw in the wilderness a large tree push over by a large man-made machine. The tree roots were exposed, and the tree trunk had water on its bark as though the tree was crying. I stopped and stared at the tree; I could feel and see the tree crying because of the exposed roots, which disconnected the tree viens for its life sourced the earth.

Just went through hurricane Sally and you can see trees fallen with roots exposed like, pine, oak, ceder, hickory and maple, not one Palm tree up rooted and root exposed you might see some dead leaves fallen but Ms Palm is still standing .

The key to life is being a palm tree instead of an oak, men are an oak tree, women are palm trees. Her based idea is on her flexibility in life and for life. She is the palm trees which never fight the wind when storms in life arise, she bends and flows to survive. Oaks, on the other hand, stand tall and firm but eventually break. Please don't get it twisted, she can be an oak tree if deemed necessary but she's mostly a palm tree.

"It's better to light a candle than to cures the darkness"

John F. Kennedy.

We own nothing of worth to present to God but ourselves. It is our ultimate sacrifice, giving God back the very life God gave to us; through woman. It's our purpose and the reason we were created to love one another, and all the living things which provide life. Now you can see where her strengths come from thy God!

Sincerely, Your Richard Dexter Russell

I asked God many times how to write this book and all of my books without education in scholastic literature. God said these words, be still and listen when I talk, read the words I wrote for you in my Holy books and Know that I'm God.

God spoke again and said in his still voice: didn't I give the birds the voice to sing, didn't I give birds their wings, didn't I give voice to the wind, didn't I give life to the water and in the streams, didn't I give water tears to cry. Didn't I create it all, and I won't let you fall, so be still and know I have given you the will to write. And your how too in life is answered in me.

Some of you may not like what I wrote, just maybe you don't understand. See God placed on my heart to write this book, and God will be done if not me, then who? You never know what's in a man's head until it moves to his heart as he writes.

You have been on such a fruitful journey reading my book. We've learned or maybe I have learned more than anyone that women are the way we communicate to the Maker of the Universe in love.

Please know and understand God not only hears us, but God also responds in his time and offers us her. She's the symbol granted us access in healing, wisdom, discernment, peace, protection, joy, and love. So much power she's willing to share, because God knew we could never handel's on our own. This is my last book in this series, I hope I have shared specific ideas and educational doctrine that can drastically change your life.

We can close out this book series together which gives a new revelation about women. By praying and reading together over time I'm hoping you can start experiencing the benefit of prayer and women today. Words are more than a paragraph, chapters and pages because words matter. By changing negative thoughts which will consist of positive results which can turn bad into good. God and women have power to direct the course of our lives. There's so much hatred in the world and I hope and pray I've done enough to show love trump hate!

Although she is the mother of nature, giving a lifetime of love and abundance thereof. Don't you love it when you can clearly see God's hand at work? It might be through an answered prayer, or a word you receive from Him. But God's hand is at work all the time in women.

God's angels called Divine Creations because God made them more special. He created them with much power as they perform different characteristics in a special place where they belong.

In my opinionated-opinion God's angels is called Woman, what an Amazing creation by God in his Glorious name with honour Extremely beautiful beings who's the light of the world.

Psalm 8:5, NIV: "You have made them a little lower than the angels and crowned them with glory and honor."

I think God has given us womens as Mother(Maa, mumma, mom, mommy) as Angel in our life. Many times you can feel this, she knows everything. no one can know you better than her. just like God she is always with you.

She is a wife, a mother, grandma, stepmom, in some cases, mother and father, an auntie, she can cook, and she can dance. She has a good sense of humor with spiritual guidance and is highly intelligent. She is able to relate to everyone. What you see is what you want!

I never felt worthy of the task God gave me. I still wonder why God chose me as the author about his mother and all women. I know the day when I meet God in Heaven, God will tell me why I was chosen.

By the way my dear readers just in case you haven't noticed, I'm a person of Christian faith the only way I could have written this book. Based fully on my Christianity beliefs and faith in women and God's grace.

Women were consistently devalued and denigrated throughout most of there's lives but, in my book, she reigned supreme. Women continue to find ways around the obstacles placed in their path or forged new paths when a challenge proved too great.

Life is unfair to some women but it does not mean it would always remain unfair.Time changes and remember every dog has its day. We all have struggles in our lives. Believe in God and His process and trust your journey. Do not give up!

The book is upholding and encouraging the understanding that women are more valuable than men, I deliver some important concessions in recognizing the value of women is, equally important, ruling that women are as individuals of values and not just a man's possession.

What made me become an Christian who writes about Christ and women?

I can give you two explanations, one long and one short. Here's the short version; without God and Christ and women, what else do we have?

The longer version; Look, I know some extreme believers in God, and women will devour my explanation and some maybe reasons with my comment. But, for those who are a bit unmerciful, please wait until the end.

Well, let's go back in time . . .

In my childhood, I used to pray to God and Jesus everyday and for his merciful love. There was a time I would imagine feeding Jesus sweets with my own hands waiting for him to eat, but God never did so. Ultimately, the sweet was eaten by me. Because God wanted me to have them. Anyways, I used to go to church with my grandmother, I watched as she prayed. And I learn to talk to God in the church and sometimes, in my mind.

My grandmother soon bought me a small wooden cross. I was so happy and excited. I wore my cross school everyday and every problem will be sorted out, especially the bad ones. I used to study for the exam and then requested my cross to give me good grades. I actually got good grades too. My cross was always present around my neck. I always take my cross with me, my symbol of God's goodness.

As I grew up, I started observing people around me which I never paid attention to earlier. I saw women in stores buying food items, milk, eggs to offer the family. But, what I saw outside the church on the street, were people asking for food and money.

They were malnourished and seemed to me on the verge of losing faith and hope. Most people were ignoring them except women and children. I observed one little girl give some money to a homeless person and he replied, "May God, bless you". You see, most people always tend to need and want someone or something whom they can talk to and share there's problems with. whom they want to follow, whom they want to idolize. In short, Faith and hope. For me it's God and women!

Well, the answer for me was simple, the only religion which I have been taught till now, on which I have read stories till now, on which I have attended religious conferences till now. I mean, why will I target other religion's, I know nothing about. Let people from there's religion question it. And to be honest, Christianity is perhaps the most interesting religion in my opinion.

Also, my answer doesn't imply my book is fake and should maybe not be followed. But in fact, there are great books to gain knowledge about religion and women. I'm attempting to write another one about her life, motivational struggles. We can learn a lot from them. But according to me, they are just amazing books written by someone brilliant. So don't simply assume these are God's Words but messages from God.

Women, true characteristics are incomprehensible to us as men. But we try to capture a small aspect of her nature through love.

Another thing I want to say is that, I'm a man, so let me believe what I want to believe. I am happy with knowing nothing else matters to me but God and women. If you realized, and think I'm wrong in my beliefs, that's your opinion. In the end, I can just say, God did it!

I hope I've proved that women are capable of ruling nations, and they could do it with intelligence, grace, love and sometimes brutality. But much of what we know about her—and don't know—about women comes from history that has been fictionalized, re-fictionalized, and fictionalized some more, so much that the made-up stuff is sometimes better-known than the facts, themselves which is kind of surprising, you think!

The unique thing about writing and seeking God and women's approval, you keep asking yourself is there is not enough you could ever do to earn God's approval. But you never stop trying. It is also a relief when I regress because the burden sometimes gets harder, but I push on . But the weight going through life wondering if you have done enough to earn God's approval, is rewarding and questionable . OMG, that pressure isn't too great not wanting to carry on to finish the books and let God and women receive the Glory.

"God's Word tells us that people are wise if they teach their mouth and add learning to their lips". Words from my book I've been given the gift to write by almighty God to write this.

If you don't like what you read, take it up with GOD! If you do like it, take it up with HIM! Because you can never know what you don't; But when you do now what?

It's my dire hope and prayer that I have created a piece of art which has moved you to tears. My book was at the mercy of me for years, to create a Behavioral Art of Rhythm in motion about her. The glory of God is revealed in the skies and the clouds that we see. The glory of God is also revelved on earth through-women we see. Looking into Bible Scripture, we find women's courageous exhortation, throughout the Old and New Testament, is in response to situations where her love and struggles is present.

In every word written in the book are mind instruments seeds which have the ability and potential to become a grown tree, if you let it grow!

The plan of the seeds is to invoke specific qualities of understanding about her. For instance, light, life, peace, joy, love and hope. Because if you know the real inner essence of her, you will be able to make your observations about her more soulful and powerful. In other words the energy-related sound of her voice.

Our bodies are composed of a combined five elements and one of them is sound.

"Studies of sound symbolism generally suggest that all vocal sounds have their meaning whether you are aware of them or not". However the sound of a woman-voice will awaken the other components elements in the body. There's numerous layers of symbolism associated with any sound. Thus, if you don't understand her, words are definitely meaningless; no vocal expression is without meaning. Isn't God Awesome! God is Capable! What a mighty God we served!

The Bible reminds us there is a time and a season for everything under heaven. This means when God has planned it, things happen when they are supposed to. Now you have finished my books. I'm hoping you would say in the same breath that Michelangelo is a true artist in the purest form, but Richard Dexter Russell is also.

From this moment on proclamations are made about women in God's eyes. The clock is set waiting for the one to hear the call and appears. God had established and put in motion my book plans, and when the time is right the plan would be executed.

Always More to Learn

This subject matter of the book, you might ask why just her, and how she got there and is there more information than could ever fit into one book. If you want to know more there is plenty more to learn and you can really take a deep dive into this topic of GODS UNFINISHED MASTERPIECE.

Whether you decide to research further or not, you can feel confident in my book you have read. I do feel this is the right message and the right time and the truth you need to know who God Masterpiece is, how much God loves you.

"I don't understand cars," Richard says. "I don't understand women. I don't understand food. I know what I enjoy. Once you try to understand something, it becomes harder to enjoy."

Thanks for choosing to buy and read my books; I'm however hoping you are awakened from the sleep of ignorance about women. The book stories were about women from the Bible and women's today, featuring the most well-known historical names and figures from Scripture's. I have compiled these stories to help you learn those whom God chose to set before us as examples of His Work.

She's a Servant OF GOD" where this hopefully life comes from. She's thrilled to be talking to someone new, by reading about her. A person camping out in the wilds reading about herself. And she envies this experience—a chance to connect with you, to rest, and to recharge, your soul as you read. She is hoping you have every intention of joining this adventurer or setting out on your own to embrace the outdoors of womanhood given by God. But she also knows you have the willpower to continue to care for family and the house and God's people. And, for her, for now, the love for God and hope and her determination to live up to what God chose for her is enough.

> "May God continue to bless you in all
> your days and all of your ways"!

> "Remember, God is never in a hurry and HE will never give up on HIS people".

> "Also, continue helping God hold up the sky."

In other words, this isn't fake news but the truth about women's made crystal clear by reality in the book. Maybe some parts of the book you could not wrap your brain around that's ok, atlases you are thinking?

The book features are so big that the researching became convincing it would be just one part of a truly massive book. But the book dating during this time may be proven controversial. This is the first time that a book of this caliber has been written and found many correlation descriptions written about women. The most fascinating thing about the word WOMAN isn't a rare phenomenon word spoken across every other language but isn't respected! The word WOMAN is "bearing the sword"—serving as a servant—in the service of society and the greater good for humanity.

Now you have finished reading the book, I hope you have a little better understanding of the women. This will help you understand why I wrote these books, someone has to!

When you begin to step away from the book storyline you begin to move towards the truth within the stories, then something happens. The understanding and celebrations of what happened as you have read. The atmosphere is completely different now. This is the focus of my writing, helping you reconcile with the truth about God's Unfinished Masterpiece.

> That's all for now; thanks for letting me into your life once again.

I do feel my book is a tool of power and a tool for power. These words and sound are formidable and they are definitely seeds that will work. Women showed amazing drive and a goal-oriented approach to solving dilemmas. Despite what women had to go through, God still triumphed in there's life and used her to bring peace and love into the world.

One of the wonderful things about writing these books is that while I was writing God changed my thinking about HIS MASTERPIECE. GOD would often leave me refocusing on positive qualities women's possession and not negatively. God would redirect things like my drive, passion, towards her natural skills and abilities in a direction that honors her in my books. That's why women are great, long before I wrote these books and still remains great after you finished reading. I learned God didn't remove her skills, but retools them for His purpose and His glory.

Later, at the conclusion of the book I hope as a writer I brought the women of the book into view. Fascinatingly, these women collectively are named the children of God. The Lord mercifully brought restoration into her life and her family.

I know I was destined to be here at this time and at this moment in my life to write this book. The journey in writing this book changed my life forever and I hope it changes yours too. I have compiled these stories to help you study those whom God chose to set before us as examples in God Word. May their lives and walks with God strengthen your knowledge and understanding and encourage your soul.

PS: It's my opinion my books may be taken out of context. But the point of my book is to incorporate stories of brave women and teach all children when they are young to understand how equally powerful women are. I laid out how gloriously powerful women are in my books and stories, so therefore children in their young minds, won't think men are always the heroes. And women are just meek creatures needing protection. There needs to be a change in our education system, that teaches our children about glorious heroic women like the one in my book and the ones you know. And I can't wait to see how people in the comments section may take the book reading to a different level of misunderstanding.

No matter what is going on in your life, remember God is always at work in your life. God is still weaving a beautiful tapestry; because she's not finished, but is in progress. Know that God is gracious, good, and that He loves you. If you find yourself discouraged on this journey called life, read about the life of women in the Bible and my books, remember God works for the good of His people.

> "Each time a woman stands up for herself, without knowing it possibly, without claiming it, she stands up for all women."~Maya Angelou

Her stories remind us that passion, commitment, love, hope and the power of God are the keys to reaching your goals in life.

All women are still within us in the idea of the divine breath that animates the flesh; and in the notion of spiritual inspiration, excitement, love, courage, caring and joy all things that are good to her are works of art.

"God's Unfinished Masterpiece." With this statement, she deserves self-respect in the face of mistreatment by those who dismiss her limitations, or neglect or truly doubt her values. The main reasons why I believe and know women are God's Masterpiece of Creation which is Unfinished. Because the earliest most profound influence was the miracle of childbirth. Ancient man was amazed how she could reproduce herself. At first the man did not think he contributed to the conception or did he? He didn't believe he was attributed to something so supernatural and mysterious as childbirth .

Soon he began seeing his woman as the source of the mystery and elevated her to the status of a goddess, his first sightful Goddess. She often wore skirts, earrings, make up and hair in place, to attract the natural protective sensuality of women as well as show her love for her man, who always accompanied her.

She is portrayed in the kneeling position, signifying the birthing position, a sacred charge, which only she can perform. Many Portraits symbolize the woman as the giver of life and nurturer of the family and the community.

She is loved yet feared but never subordinated.

The following paragraph demonstrates and confirms that although man is awed by women, he can only dream of her being unfinished.

I'm trying to reinforce her values throughout the book by highlighting the often-overlooked contributions of women. In doing so, don't forget to embrace women of color for the reality of their struggle, while inspiring others with the determination to overcome obstacles.

It can resonate with anyone, my true friends who support and encourage you to be your best self. May God continue to Bless you in all your days and all your ways.

I've traveled lonely roads as a writer but my journey has been with you. My prayer for my book is to inspire us to do whatever goodness in life to help others regardless of the challenges. And have as much determination as you want, to reach your goals. You have to take the first step even though the steps may become difficult, to reach your goals.

> "Make decisions based on what should happen, not what shouldn't"?
> By Michelle Obama

Now let words alone be clear and translucent like glass, especially in smooth seas clearly or in an unclear sky. Women mentioned in my book have been the subject of poems, paintings and even stained-glass art pieces. In all religious faiths, she has been observed in her honor, along with other women who were very active in ministry for the early church. The many stories written in my of these Godly women offer insights for Christians who want to make a real difference in their families and communities.

God has always gifted women to bring positive change to their surroundings, and family who was obedient to the call on her life. Women in the books are still a wonderful example of what it means to submit our talents to the Lord, and to leave a legacy behind. And God will always multiply the blessings that come from selfless giving.

My name is Richard Dexter Russell and I approve of the reading of this book!

In the book I'm giving you objectives, illustrations and situations to build up and explain God's love for His Masterpiece, for you to understand who she is in the eyes of God. Understand my dear readers I didn't make a deal with God to write about her God told me to write about her. You don't make deals with God you do what you are told.

I have read and research the treatment of girl's and women while I was there in my studying the young lady and women weren't in most cases treated with respect and dignity. They were bullied, discriminated against, physically, sexually and verbally abused. She's also been put down talked about trying to deminished her but she never lost her values in the eyes of God. Because her values are definitely not determined by man but by God, shes not the child of man but the woman of God.

She's the (Bearer of Heavens created by God) God personified her quality of endurance to be Unfinished Masterpiece.

Women's System of beliefs:

Woman is an unfinished masterpiece of God's creations. She is a metamorphic co-creator. It is hard to comprehend her nature. She camouflages to fit situations and test of times, a mysteries being created to take the shape of the ideal creations. Men describe her as admirable, delightful, beautiful, magnetic, and radiant and confidant. Children look at her as their cornerstone. The bible exemplifies woman as a builder, destroyer, pillar, city, Church, and the manipulator.

As a system of belief, the story considers a woman as a symbol of a nation of Israel. Also, a woman will be represented by Babylon. The old and new covenant is equated to a woman by Isaiah 47. A woman is also the church illustrating the practices and the beliefs in Christianity. A Woman represented the unfinished work of bringing sanity to the world. The moral guidelines and dimensions are ingrained in a woman. The real-life example is that she's awesome.

The story of the woman will be guided by the women's who bled for years. The woman that stood beside Jesus Christ in His ministry. Also, women that are in the bible of the bride and the bridegroom.

Woman the pillar:

A woman is universally respected. She is hardworking, reliable, and decent. Women engage in giving and voluntary work. It is common to encounter women taking care of their neighbour's dog or children. Men consider women as the pillar of families. The traditional setting predisposes a woman to the position of a builder and pillar. Examples of stories where women performed roles in the absent of the husband. The story recounts on the world wars and single woman parenting.

The story is equivalent to the women that supported Jesus in His ministry. The women that played the role of queens and kings in destroying or rectifying reigns. Women that brought change and salvation in the world.

Woman the Co-creator:

Finally, a woman is a co-creator with God. She continues with God's work of creation by giving birth. The story explains the nature of women in giving birth and taking care of children. More description is given on the purpose of the female gender and why it was important. Through co-creation salvation is brought to the world.

Woman the co-creator nature of women is equivalent to the role played by the Mary mother of Jesus and Elizabeth, her cousin. Also, the story examines the story of Sara and her role in bringing forth a blessed generation.

The women of scripture I am writing about I've found an encouraging and honorably calling to pursue God intention in their stories of strong faith. The stories of these women have a deep impact on my life. And, for the record, I'm a man writing about women and I am hoping and praying she's not offended.

Men: If you don't have a woman hero to look up to, I'll have few names; your mother, sister, grandmother, greatgrandmother, and Aunties. If the women in your family isn't enough keep reading you're looking in the right place. Just hold-on your life is about to change.

Ladies: While gender-equality is a controversial subject for some men (honestly, I don't understand why), it's their fault, because it has never been with God. If you've ever been looked over, pushed aside, or made to feel less-than or not equal. I'm sorry about that but they didn't know you were God's chosen.

God routinely used women in incredible ways to advance his plans on earth, and God still doing it today.

Everyone: Need a blueprint for a meaningful life? In my book are my chosen 12 of the most wonderful women written to reflect the many women from the Bible. When you find one woman you connect with in stories you recognize, she will reminds you of someone.

You just might met your next favorite hero, and in the process, encounter that'd she's behind all God's calling upon us.

NOW you can see, wonder women in reality not in comic books and movie screens. The stories of these women, and many others, have profoundly influenced me as a man and servant and I pray you can feel what I feel.

I'm compelled by each one to be a better student how to be(and writer and a good man), and to honor all the wonderful women in the Bible and in my life.

But that's just fine for me. The more important question is, how will these women inspire you?

If we do not meet again, my friends—
my adieu—will be but a memory
but at the very least we happened. Me and God's
Unfinished Masterpiece (Woman)